CAMPAIGN 353

BRITANNIA AD 43

The Claudian Invasion

NIC FIELDS

ILLUSTRATED BY STEVE NOON
Series editor Marcus Cowper

OSPREY PUBLISHING
Bloomsbury Publishing Plc
Kemp House, Chawley Park, Oxford OX2 9PH, UK
1385 Broadway, 5th Floor, New York, NY 10018, USA
29 Earlsfort Terrace, Dublin 2, Ireland
www.ospreypublishing.com

OSPREY is a trademark of Osprey Publishing,

First published in Great Britain in 2020

© Osprey Publishing, 2020 – Email: info@ospreypublishing.com

A catalogue record for this book is available from the British Library.

ISBN: PB 9781472842077; eBook 9781472842084; ePDF 9781472842053;
XML 9781472842060

21 22 23 24 25   10 9 8 7 6 5 4 3 2

Maps by bounford.com
3D BEVs by Paul Kime
Index by Sandra Shotter
Typeset by PDQ Digital Media Solutions, Bungay, UK
Printed and bound by Bell & Bain Ltd., Glasgow G46 7UQ.

Artist's note

Readers may care to note that the original paintings from which the colour
plates in this book were prepared are available for private sale. All
reproduction copyright whatsoever is retained by the publishers. The artist
can be contacted via the following website:

https://www.steve-noon.co.uk

The publishers regret that they can enter into no correspondence upon
this matter.

Osprey Publishing supports the Woodland Trust, the UK's leading woodland
conservation charity.

To find out more about our authors and books visit
www.ospreypublishing.com. Here you will find extracts, author
interviews, details of forthcoming events and the option to sign up for
our newsletter.

Key to military symbols

xxxxx	xxxx	xxx	xx	x	III	II
Army Group	Army	Corps	Division	Brigade	Regiment	Battalion

I				
Company/Battery	Infantry	Artillery	Cavalry	**Key to unit identification**

Key to unit identification

Unit identifier — Parent unit — Commander
(+) with added elements
(–) less elements

PREVIOUS PAGE
Members of the Praetorian Guard, from the Arch of Claudius,
erected in honour of the successful invasion of Britannia. (Carole
Raddato/Wikimedia Commons/CC-BY-SA-2.0)

CONTENTS

The Roman Empire at the death of Augustus

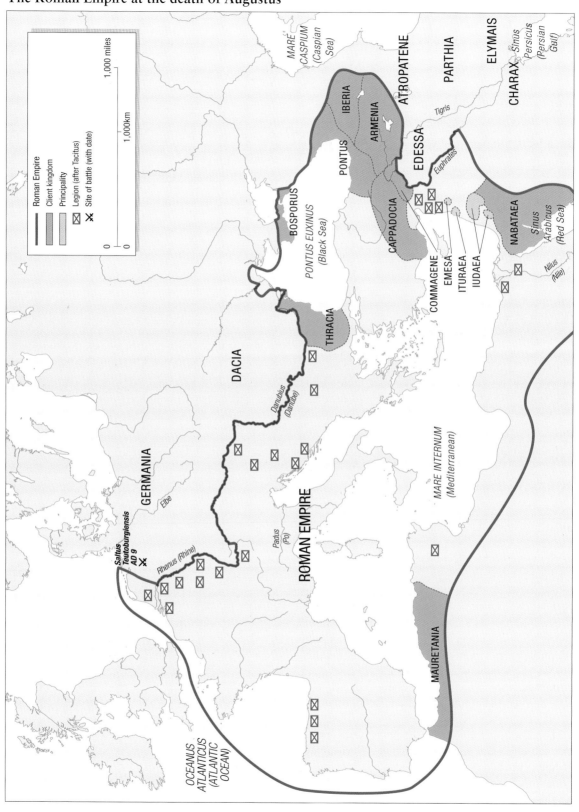

MARE CASPIUM (Caspian Sea)

ATROPATENE

PARTHIA

ELYMAIS

CHARAX

Sinus Persicus (Persian Gulf)

IBERIA

ARMENIA

PONTUS

EDESSA

Tigris

Roman Empire
Client kingdom
Principality
Legion (after Tacitus)
Site of battle (with date)

1,000 miles

1,000km

BOSPORUS

CAPPADOCIA

COMMAGENE

EMESA

ITURAEA

IUDAEA

Euphrates

NABATAEA

Sinus Arabicus (Red Sea)

PONTUS EUXINUS *(Black Sea)*

Nilus (Nile)

THRACIA

DACIA

Danubius (Danube)

GERMANIA

Elbe

MARE INTERNUM *(Mediterranean)*

Saltus Teutoburgiensis AD 9

Rhenus (Rhine)

Padus (Po)

ROMAN EMPIRE

MAURETANIA

OCEANUS ATLANTICUS (ATLANTIC OCEAN)

ORIGINS OF THE CAMPAIGN

BRITANNIA BC

The oldest name of the largest island of the British Isles known to us is Albion (Celtic or pre-Celtic), first recorded in the 1st century AD, by when it had been superseded (among Romans) by Britannia (e.g. Plin. *HN* 4.102). The Latin name, perhaps, derives from that used by the Greeks, namely Pretanníā. As early as the 4th century BC, the Greek colony of Massilia (Marseille) knew of the existence of Pretanníā, and sometime about 320 BC saw a partial exploration by one of its citizens. This was Pytheas, a man whose many-sided talents can be illustrated from the fact that he was at once a sailor, merchant, observational scientist, astronomer and explorer, to whom we owe the earliest written account of the British Isles. On his return home to the civilized Mediterranean world, the intrepid Pytheas wrote a book, *Tà perì toũ Okeanoũ*, now lost apart from passing references in Strabo (1.4.3, 2.4.1, 2.5.8, 4.4.1, 4.5.5) amongst others.

Caesarian overture
It could be said that one of his greatest traits as a general – *celeritas*, quickness of action – was to become a burden. Yet Caius Iulius Caesar was an adventurer and showman who could not resist the lure of the unknown, the unknown being Britannia, of course. Some battles were fought, some settlements burnt and some hostages taken. Back home the publicity was excellent, as Britannia was represented as 'beyond the Oceanus', which had certainly stifled the ambitions of Alexander the Great. Even Cicero (*QFr.* 2.14.2) had been caught up in the hype, planning to write an epic poem addressed to Caesar on his 'glorious conquest', based on front-line reports from his brother Quintus, who was serving as one of Caesar's *legati* (deputies). Apparently, it was eventually finished (ibid. 3.7.4).

With a much better prepared plan of campaign, Caesar returned to Britannia with over half of his army currently operating in Gaul: five legions – VII, X Equestris, possibly XIIII, and two others – and 2,000 auxiliary cavalry. He landed unopposed at what is now Ebbsfleet, near Ramsgate (Fitzpatrick 2018, 2019), reached the river Thames and defeated Cassivellaunus of the Catuvellauni. The aggressive behaviour of the Catuvellauni, a Gallo-Belgic tribe, towards its neighbouring tribes had already become a cause for concern, and in the nine decades prior to the Roman occupation, they would be the most successful of all the tribes of southern Britannia.

Iulius Caesar memorial, Kentish costal town of Walmer. Caesar's first foray into Britannia came in late August 55 BC, when he landed on a shingle beach somewhere between Walmer and Sandwich, beyond the White Cliffs of Dover (in *B Gall.* 4.23.9 he describes the landing site as *aperto ac plano*, 'open and even'), with *legiones* VII and X Equestris. The aquilifer of Legio X Equestris leapt into the sea alone, holding the shaft of the unit's gilded eagle grasping a thunderbolt in its talons. His impetuous action prompted the hesitant men of the invasion force to follow his rash example and drive the waiting Cantiaci back from the foreshore. (Neddyseagoon/ Wikimedia Commons/ CC-BY-SA-3.0)

Caesar's brief campaigns in Britannia are, of course, open to various interpretations. His *commentarii* were at least partially available in Rome soon after the events, and served not only as a report on his progress, but were also meant to further his political career. Thus, at one level he was playing to the Roman gallery by crossing the Oceanus and setting foot in a land of mystery; but curiosity, not least about the rumoured mineral wealth of the islands, may have provided an incentive. As Caesar says himself in his fourth *commentarius*, 'in an ordinary way no one goes to Britannia except traders [*mercatores*], and even they are acquainted only with the seacoast and the areas that are opposite Gaul' (*B Gall.* 4.20.3). Though the expense of garrisoning Britannia would have probably outweighed the potential profits – Rome expected its provinces to pay for themselves – limited conquest may have been an option. In the event, however, he left after having established some form of treaty relations with the Trinovantes, and probably other tribes, in the region north of the Thames.

Sometime in the autumn of 54 BC, Cicero had written the following in a letter to his close friend Atticus:

> On 24 October, I received letters from my brother Quintus and Caesar dispatched from 'Shores of Nearer Britannia, 25 September'. They had settled Britannia, taken hostages but no booty (tribute, however, imposed), and were bringing back the army from the island. (Cic. *Att.* 4.18.5)

You can almost feel the air of disappointment and anticlimax as Cicero writes those two words *nulla praeda*, 'no booty'. It should not be forgotten, in the ancient world, that wars of conquest usually showed a handsome profit for the victor. Lack of profit notwithstanding, from an objective military point of view, Caesar's two expeditions over the Oceanus were rash in conception, hasty and ill-advised in execution, in fact near-disasters. The fact that he committed more than half of his army to the second expedition was a great gamble, when Gaul was only newly conquered and its tribes still in a rebellious mood. And so it was, the great gambler was forced to retreat to Gaul to deal with problems there before the winter weather broke.

Still, Caesar being Caesar was able to spin his limited victories as a conquest of sorts, planting the flag as opposed to leaving boots on the ground. It worked, for the second expedition to this seemingly remote region was heralded as a great triumph in the centre of power, Rome itself, though it seems there were a few dissenting voices. Take, for instance, the spiteful statement penned by Lucan, when he has Pompeius Magnus summarize Caesar's exploits in his epic poem *Pharsalia*. Caesar – the hero of his own *commentarii* – not only is shamed, but made to look absolutely ridiculous when a sneering Pompeius plunges the knife deeper and twists, for his rival in warlordism *territa quaesitis ostendit terga Britannis*, 'came looking for the Britons and then terrified, turned tail' (2.572). Strong stuff, but admittedly written a hundred years or so after the event.

The contact period

Writing to his only brother Quintus, some four years his junior, Cicero was appalled at the prospect of his brother's crossing to Britannia in 54 BC. In one letter to Quintus, written from Rome in late August of that year, he gave vent to his relief at his brother's safe landing in Britannia:

> How I was pleased to get your letter from Britannia! I dreaded the Oceanus and the island coast. Not that I make light of what is to come, but there is more to hope than to fear, and my suspense is more a matter of anticipation than of anxiety. (Cic. *QFr.* 2.16.3)

For the Romans, the island of Britannia lay far beyond the comfortable confines of the bright and beautiful Mediterranean world. This was the middle world around which classical civilization had formed and flourished, 'like frogs around a pond' (Pl. *Phd.* 109b) as Plato famously quipped. Britannia was felt to be a dark and uninviting place at the outermost edge of the world itself, a fact that lent this island outpost of the habitable world an air of dangerous mystique in the eyes of the Greek and Roman literati.

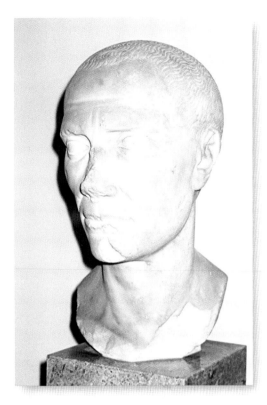

Marble bust (Museo Archeologico Regionale, Palermo, inv. NI 1967) of Caius Iulius Caesar, Iulio-Claudian copy of a 1st-century BC original, provenance unknown. His first invasion of Britannia in the late summer of 55 BC was ostensibly in reprisal for Britannic aid to the Gauls, but Caesar was also a master showman and his crossing of the Oceanus caused great excitement in Rome. The invasion actually achieved very little other than almost losing the Roman fleet in a storm. He was to repeat the performance on a grander scale the following year, which was to result in the first real contact with the insular tribes of southern mainland Britannia. (© Nic Fields)

The Augustan poet Virgil described the inhabitants of Britannia, some six decades before the Claudian invasion, as 'wholly sundered from the world' (*Ecl.* 1.66). Much later Roman writers would shrug Britannia off as an out-of-the-way place, set apart as it was in the boundless Oceanus, with its inaccessible shores, treacherous tides and mists no sun could penetrate, and stiff with ice all winter – a new and frightening world entirely. Bizarrely, this feeling of remoteness continued right up to the very end of the Roman occupation some four centuries later, when contemporary writers would still talk as if Britannia had only been discovered or conquered in recent memory.

The *topos* of the remoteness of Britannia may have been commonplace in Greek and Latin literature, but this was an isolation more romantic than real. Britannia, invaded briefly by Caesar on two occasions, remained free, but in contact with the Roman world. As Tacitus says:

> The deified Iulius [Caesar] was indeed the first Roman to enter Britannia with an army, but though he intimidated the inhabitants by a victory and gained control of the coast, it is clear he merely pointed it out to those who came after him; he did not bequeath it to them. (Tac. *Agr.* 13.2)

The island, though pedalled as being close to the edge, did not exist *in vacuo*, for there is solid evidence to show that chieftains in the south and east of Britannia had political links with Rome. And that was not all. Merchants from Gaul and the Mediterranean world (principally Massiliotes, and occasionally Italians or Romans) had already gained a firm hold in southern and eastern regions of the mainland island. As a result, a trickle of luxury goods came into these regions of Britannia from the Mediterranean, and they spoke of affluence and allure, and a much wider world.

The tumulus of a local noble a kilometre or so west of central Colchester, the Lexden Tumulus (as it is known), contained not only a number of small copper alloy figures imported from Italy, but also a silver medallion of Augustus. This had been made by cutting out the bust of the emperor from a Roman denarius minted in 17 BC, which was then soldered onto a silver disc and put into a moulded frame. Amongst the grave goods were at least 17 wine amphorae, sheet alloy and cast fittings representing a casket or chest, fused chunks of a mail shirt decorated with silver studs and with bronze hinges and a folding stool similar to those used by Roman magistrates. All in all, it is a thoroughly Romanized assemblage, all of it imported, and clearly belonged to a man of great importance. It has been suggested that the individual concerned may have been Addedomaros, a king of the Trinovantes, a tribe controlling the area that we now know as the county of Essex and much of the county of Suffolk.

Coins were first introduced to Britannia by the Belgic incomers, and the first identifiable coinage to emerge in this area is that of Addedomaros, dating to around 35 BC. He issued gold staters (Greek: στατήρ, 'weight'), as well as a range of silver and bronze coinage. Other local nobles soon followed suit, minting their own silver and bronze coins, patterned on Roman types, some with the title equivalent to the Latin *rex*, emphasising their position as king of the tribe.

A native noble burial dated *c.* AD 20/30 from the funerary site found at the Essex village of Stanway, some 5km west of central Colchester, contained imported Roman consumer goods, including a fine set of 24 Roman plates and drinking vessels. Other finds include large quantities of imported amphorae (mainly Italian, but some from Iberia), used to bring in olive oil and wine. The amphorae themselves are not particularly impressive, but they do include the type known as Dressel 1B, which was made principally along the Tyrrhenian coastal area of Italy from Etruria to Campania, and seems to be associated, by and large, with the high-quality white wines of the Caecuban and Falernian plains.[1] Caecuban (Cæcubum) and Falernian (Falernum) wines were extolled by the Augustan poet Horace (*Epod.* 1.20.9–10, 1.37.5, 2.3.7–8, 2.11.19,

---

1   Amphorae were above all containers for seaborne trade. Their shape with its pointed bottom was ideally suited for lifting, emptying and stacking the amphorae in a ship's hull. Their capacity varied on average from 25 to 30 litres; the resulting weight of some 35kg, when the amphora was full, was a convenient weight for carrying.

Sat. 2.4.24), a man who knew his wines. While the site of Camulodunum–Colchester has been shown by extensive excavation to have been entirely Roman, the funerary site at Stanway, by contrast, is a short distance west of the Iron Age centre located at Gosbecks. Gosbecks is probably where the emperor Claudius accepted the surrender of 11 Britannic kings – more on which later.

THE ORIGINS OF THE CLAUDIAN CAMPAIGN

Caius Iulius Caesar Augustus Germanicus, to give Caligula his proper name, the great-nephew of Tiberius, the son of a military hero, and himself an idol (almost a mascot) of the army, never set foot in Britannia, so much is certain, as is the fact that he was hailed by the army as Britannicus, the victor over Britannia. According to Suetonius (*Calig.* 44-7) and Cassius Dio (59.21.3, 25.1–3), in AD 39 Caius Caligula went to Gaul, and after initial preparations, engaged in military activities against the trans-Rhenish Germanic tribes, for which he was saluted as *imperator* seven times (Dio 59.22.2), before progressing the following spring to the Oceanus. There, on the seashore, he commanded his soldiers to collect sea shells, in their helmets and the folds of their tunics, as the *spoila Oceani*, 'spoils over the Oceanus' (Suet. *Calig.* 46). Was he mocking his men for refusing to invade Britannia? Orosius, writing in the early 5th century AD, says *deficiente belli materia*, 'Because he lacked the supplies for war' (7.5.5), perhaps a plausible excuse. Caligula then had a lighthouse built, likened to the Pharos of Alexandria, whose location is not specified (Suet. *Calig.* 46); it has been suggested it was either located at Gesoriacum–Boulogne-sur-Mer, or somewhere near the estuary of the Rhine. On his return to Rome, he celebrated his military victories over Germania and Britannia. Caligula was no general, nor could he by any stretch of the imagination be said to have won any military victories during his two northern campaigns.

This episode, one of the most celebrated ventures of his reign, has provided much grist to the academic mill. Of course, without further evidence, it will probably never be possible to get to the truth of what really happened in AD 40 on the shores of the Oceanus facing Britannia. As Tacitus says, the fact that 'Caius Caesar debated an invasion of Britannia is well known; but his sensitivities were quick to repent: besides, his vast designs against Germania had failed' (*Agr.* 13). As a military commander, Caligula left a great deal to be desired. Nevertheless, he did formulate the plans for the conquest of Britannia, which would be put into effect by his successor three years later.

Born to rule
It was this pursuit of an erratic foreign policy that was to be his undoing. Caius Caligula had already alienated the Jews in Alexandria and elsewhere for no good reason other than his increasing conviction of his own divinity. Now his farcical foray into Germania, that

Bronze head (British Museum, London, inv. P&EE 1965 12-1 1) of a life-size equestrian statue of Claudius, found (1907) in the bed of the Alde at Rendham, near Saxmundham in Suffolk. A jagged line around the neck shows where it had been violently hacked from the torso. It is believed to have been looted from Camulodunum–Colchester during its sack by the rebel alliance led by Boudica. Like the *tête coupée*, it may have been thrown in the Alde in fulfilment of some ritual imperative. Seventeen years earlier, matters had been very different: a striking military victory that initiated the full-scale annexation of Britannia as a province and gave Claudius the authority he needed to secure his throne. He was the first to bring the barbarians beyond the Oceanus under the direct rule of Rome, and this achievement was clearly regarded by him as the culmination of the campaigns of his famous forebear Iulius Caesar begun 97 years before. (Carole Raddato/Wikimedia Commons/CC-BY-SA-2.0)

availed nothing, was to be immediately followed by all the preparations for a major invasion of Britannia, which was then inexplicably called off at the last minute. Such failures did not endear him to the army. The tipping point came when his wayward behaviour invited the wrath of the Praetorian Guard. The emperor's days were numbered.

Universally hailed as the New Sun shedding light on a world that had been plunged into tyrannical darkness, Caligula's reign had started well, and he seemed to have the makings of a popular emperor – although his initial popularity must have been because of the memory of his father Germanicus, rather than any perceived merits of Caligula. He had been raised to the purple by the manoeuvrings of Macro, 'self-made' man and the prefect of the Praetorians; the Senate was presented with a fait accompli. Whatever reservations there might have been about the legality of Caligula's position, there could be no doubt that, in practical terms, he was in control. Caligula moved quickly to win friends by a shrewd mixture of theatrical gestures and sound practical measures. He abolished the sales tax, restored the elections to the people, recalled those exiled during the reign of Tiberius (including actors), suppressed the use of paid informers and stopped the treason trials. He gave splendid public spectacles and shows, winning the adoration of the ordinary people of Rome. On his accession, Caligula's conduct was exemplary, and this probably continued for six months or so (Philo *Leg.* 2.13). But that is a whole other story.

The emperor's pattern of grandiosity, delusions of godhead, profound entitlement, insufferable arrogance, desperate need for attention (if not worship) and bitter spite, all but guaranteed the outcome that he would not be able to resist abusing his power; and he did not. Then, Nemesis struck. Caius Caligula was whacked in a well-planned ambush by senior officers of the Praetorian Guard, while passing along the narrow cryptoporticus beneath the Palatine Hill during a series of games and dramatics being held during the Ludi Palatini (24 January AD 41). It was an end as murderous as his four-year reign, and no less gruesome.

The Praetorian Guard had not made ambitious political plans. Their purpose, quite simply, was to eliminate a tyrant. In the confusion that followed, the Praetorians began to loot Caligula's palace. As hours passed, they began to realize the political implications of their heinous act. They had butchered Caligula's wife and infant daughter, so there should be no one honour-bound by name to exact retribution. And, slowly, it dawned on them that with no emperor, there was no longer a need for a Praetorian Guard.

In the course of looting Caligula's palace, apparently some Praetorians found a 50-year-old man cowering behind some curtains, fearing for his own life. It was Tiberius Claudius Nero Germanicus, the son of Nero Claudius Drusus Germanicus, the younger brother of Tiberius, and Iulia Antonia Minor, the daughter of Marcus Antonius and Octavia Minor. He was also uncle to Caligula, whose rollercoaster reign he had survived by 'playing ball with the Mad King'. Since birth, Claudius had suffered from a number of congenital defects. The cause might be any number of things, but almost predictably, the symptoms are described with some relish in the literary sources. He stuttered badly, was lame or had a limp of some sort, had a tendency to drool and laugh uncontrollably, and his mind would wander so that he employed a slave whose sole job was to remind the emperor what he had been saying.

Political geography of Britannia on the eve of the Claudian invasion

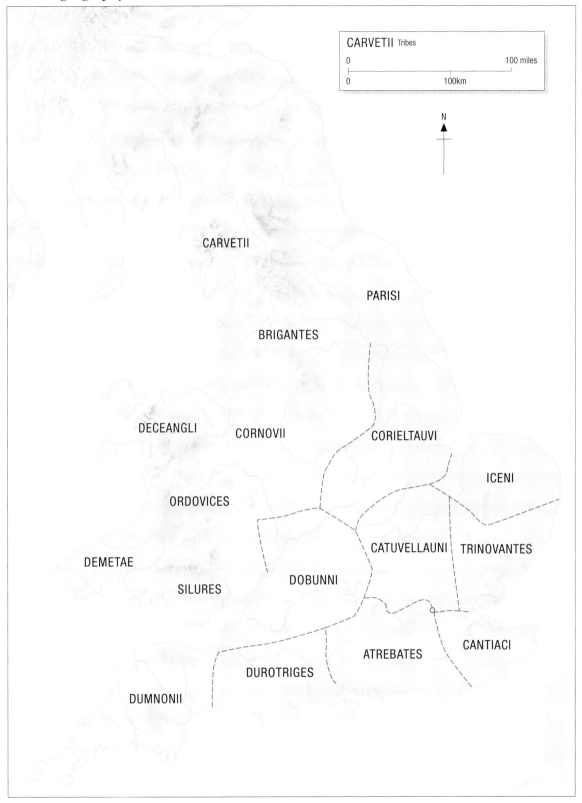

CARVETII Tribes

0   100 miles

0   100km

N

CARVETII

PARISI

BRIGANTES

DECEANGLI   CORNOVII

CORIELTAUVI

ICENI

ORDOVICES

CATUVELLAUNI   TRINOVANTES

DEMETAE

DOBUNNI

SILURES

ATREBATES

CANTIACI

DUROTRIGES

DUMNONII

Thus it was that Claudius was dragged unceremoniously from his academic abstruseness to fulfil the need for a dynast of the Iulio-Claudian family. The surprised, and for the moment terrified, Claudius had never been even remotely considered as a possible successor to any emperor. He had been kept out of public life, and sought consolation in his scholarly studies, occasionally enlivened by drinking, gambling and other such self-indulgences. The most unlikely of imperial figures, his sole qualification to office was that he belonged to the imperial house, and was, indeed, virtually the only male survivor, for the simple reason that no one had ever thought it worth the trouble of executing him, poisoning him, forcing him to suicide or packing him off into exile. But this was enough for his sponsors, the soldiers of the Praetorian Guard, who at this time represented the only real military muscle in Rome.

So, the Praetorians took Claudius to the safety of the *castra praetoria* (it was more like a fortress than a camp) and hailed him as emperor, perhaps seriously, perhaps only in jest. But when they paraded the old man through the streets, and the gathering crowds likewise hailed him as emperor, the die was cast. 'Poor old Uncle Claudius', the family embarrassment, was now elevated to the purple. In the acerbic words of Edward Gibbon, 'while [the senators] deliberated, the Praetorian Guards had resolved'.[2] In the Senate, there was talk of declaring the Republic restored and dispensing with emperors altogether (Suet. *Claud.* 10.1–3, Dio 60.1.3a, Joseph. *B Iud.* 2.11.2 [206–7]). It had been a long hundred years since liberty, and the rule of law had really flourished in the Republic, from the time of the drumhead agreement between Pompeius, Crassus and Caesar, the triumvirate of 59 BC; but like Caesar's assassins, the Senate dithered.

Although it is an over-simplification to say that the Praetorians made Claudius emperor, it is true that their support was more obviously important than before – a truism that the new emperor understood when he secured their loyalty by means of a generous lump-sum payment of five years' salary, 15,000 sesterces no less (Suet. *Claud.* 10.4). Even so, Claudius' position on the throne was initially insecure, and his most obvious failing was his complete lack of military prestige. The support of the legions outside Rome was the critical element in the creation and continued support of any reign (a fact that allowed Claudius to come to power, as later it would allow Vespasianus; while losing the legions' support had disastrous effects, as Nero would learn to his cost). Additionally, the inexplicable vacillations of his unbalanced predecessor could well have been damaging to Roman prestige, so the adoption of an expansionist policy by Claudius may have been necessary to ensure that those beyond the frontiers were left with no illusion about the reality of Roman strength.

Unfinished business?

Iulius Caesar had a brilliant incisive mind, a man who had a preference for an intensely physical life of continuous movement (occasionally very rapid), making instant decisions. Caius Iulius Caesar Octavianus ('Augustus' after 16 January 27 BC), on the other hand, was quite a different person to his adoptive father. He was essentially an intellectual, whose great mental abilities were dedicated to the perfection of the state organization, which he gradually and carefully established. His decisions were usually reached after a careful

---

2   Edward Gibbon, *The History of the Decline and Fall of the Roman Empire* (abridged edition), London: Penguin, 2000, Chapter III, p. 77.

consideration of all the factors, but he held in his mind almost a total grasp of the complexities of the large, sprawling empire he ruled over. He was by nature cautious, preferring the compromise solution, and had little of the debonair brilliance of Caesar. Unlike his murdered adoptive father, the first emperor would become a quietly spoken grandfather figure, leathery and lined, a master of one-liners, a fixer, one to have a quiet word.

Bronze coin (*RPC* I 1588) struck in Thessaloniki. The obverse (left) depicts a bust of Claudius with the Greek legend TI ΚΛΑΥΔΙΟС ΚΑΙСΑΡ СΕΒΑСΤΟС, while the reverse (right) bears a bust of his son Britannicus and the Greek legend ΒΡΕΤΑΝΝΙΚΟС ΘΕССΑΛΟΝΙ. The occasion of the conquest of Britannia by the emperor was not only proclaimed on coins issued in the West, but in the East too. (Johny SYSEL/Wikimedia Commons/ CC-BY-SA-3.0)

It appears that in 34 BC, according to Cassius Dio at least, 'Augustus was pressing ahead with a Britannic expedition in emulation of his father' (49.38.2), a scheme he was to resuscitate once more in 27 BC and again the following year (ibid. 53.22.5, 25.2). The contemporary poet Horace might well implore the goddess Fortuna 'that you may protect [Augustus] on his expedition against the Britons, the furthest nation of the world' (*Epod.* 1.35.29–30, cf. 3.5.1–4), while another unknown poet was to harp on that 'there awaits [Augustus] the Briton, unconquered by Roman Mars' (*Panegyricus Messallae* 150). Nothing, however, came of it, and whether or not Augustus' intentions regarding the conquest of Britannia were at all serious, we shall never really know.

What we do know, however, is that Augustus bequeathed to Tiberius a policy of status quo, advising his adopted son and successor 'that the empire should not be extended beyond its present frontiers' (Tac. *Ann.* 1.11). What was in fact an injunction stood for nigh-on three decades, until Claudius renounced it by his invasion of AD 43. Tiberius, although he had been one of the most experienced of the commanders of Augustus' time, was to follow the mandate to the letter. A superb soldier, Tiberius evolved into a supreme general; his wars were won by strategy rather than slaughter. Conversely, there was a consciousness among other Roman commanders of a 'heroic past' that they felt drawn to emulate without being impeded by a jealous commander-in-chief. Tacitus records the verbal outburst of Cnaeus Domitius Corbulo, *legatus pro praetore* of Germania Inferior and one of the finest commanders of his day, when instructed by Claudius in AD 47 to stop further aggression against the Chauci of the north German plain: 'Earlier Roman commanders were fortunate!' (*Ann.* 11.21, cf. Dio 61.30.5).

From a military point of view, the Claudian invasion was a misguided venture, the decision to embark upon it taken against the weight of evidence. Be this as it may, one thing is certain: Rome's northern frontier could hardly have been more clearly defined or better protected than by the Oceanus. 'What wall,' Flavius Josephus later asks, 'could be a better obstacle than the open sea that is the bulwark of Britannia?' (*B Iud.* 6.6.2 [331]). Turn the question on its head, and equally it was Rome's too. The astute Augustus appreciated this, and, accordingly, had rejected the option of invasion. In the words of the Augustan geographer Strabo:

> Though Rome could have taken Britannia, it declined to do so. In the first place, the Britons are no threat, having insufficient strength to cross over and attack us. In the second, there would be little to gain. It seems that we presently get more out of them in duty on their exports than we would by direct taxation,

especially if the costs of an occupation army and of tax collecting be discounted. The same goes even more for the islands around about Britannia. (Strab. 2.5.8)

Strabo mentions too the apparent riches of Britannia when he lists the island's exports of corn, cattle, gold, silver, iron, hides, slaves and hunting dogs, all items of vital importance to the Augustan military effort on the Rhine frontier. As mentioned before, the reverse traffic is indicated by finds of mainly luxury goods in pre-conquest Britain: Roman fine pottery, amphorae for their contents like wine and olive oil, jewellery and other fine and pretty things.

One commodity of great interest for the Romans was tin. With the exception of minor deposits in Anatolia, Italy and Iberia, tin was virtually non-existent in the Mediterranean world. On the other hand, in northern Europe tin occurred naturally (as cassiterite or tin oxide) in a few locations, namely north-western Gaul and south-western Britannia. It does seem likely that from as early as the second millennium BC, tin from what is now Cornwall was being shipped to mainland Europe, potentially reaching far across Europe and hence on to the Mediterranean world. There is ample evidence for the Roman pursuit of fabulous tin, including the expedition noted by Strabo (3.5.11) of Publius Licinius Crassus: this either relates to an expedition between 96 BC and 93 BC off Iberia, or in 57 BC by the *legatus* of Caesar's Legio VII in south-western Britannia. According to Diodorus Siculus, a contemporary of Caesar and Augustus:

> The inhabitants of Britannia who dwell about the promontory of Belerion [Cornwall] are especially hospitable to strangers and have adopted a civilized manner of life because of their intercourse with merchants and other peoples … they work tin into pieces the size of knucklebones and convey it to an island off Britannia that is called Ictis [Saint Michael's Mount] … On the island, merchants purchase the tin of the natives and carry it from there across the Oceanus to Gaul; and finally, making their way on foot through Gaul for some 30 days, they bring their wares on horseback to the mouth of the river Rhodanus [Rhône]. (Diod. Sic. 5.22.1–4)

For Claudius, the temptation of Britannia lay not in strategic or fiscal advantage, but in a one-man publicity stunt and the stir which would be created in Rome by pushing the northern frontier of the empire across the 'boundless ocean'. For Claudius needed glory.

Claudius' appearance at the terminal point of the campaign, complete with a large train of personages, Praetorians and pachyderms, is quite remarkable (Dio 60.21.2–5). Though both his father Drusus and brother Germanicus had enjoyed enormous reputations as soldiers, and the latter had attained a mythical status since his untimely death under suspicious circumstances, the emperor was elderly and sickly and of a scholarly disposition. He had penned a number of historical treatises in Greek during his informative years, notably a history of the Etruscan people, the Carthaginians (Suet. *Claud.* 42.2) and in Latin a controversial account of the last civil war, namely that involving his maternal grandfather and adoptive grandfather, Marcus Antonius and Augustus respectively (ibid. 41.2). Indeed, it would be hard to imagine a more unmilitary figure. Yet he made the long and arduous journey from Rome to Britannia, and returned in six months for a splendid triumph.

A plausible pretext

The essentials of the story are easily told. A plausible excuse for the invasion seems to have been to aid an aging expatriate Britannic prince known as Verica, who had been recognized as *rex* of the Atrebates by Rome, a Gallo-Belgic tribe who inhabited a kingdom corresponding roughly to the later counties of Hampshire, West Sussex and Berkshire. He was either the son or grandson of Commius, the very same Commius who had initially assisted, and then resisted, Caesar during his conquest of Gaul. Having taken on Caesar in Gaul and lost, he ended up taking refuge in Britannia.

'Hidden Faces' gold stater of Tasciovanus of the Catuvellauni. The obverse (left) bears stylized crescents and wreaths with hidden faces, while the reverse (right) depicts a Celtic warrior carrying carnyx on a horse. Tasciovanus minted a large number of different coin types, and extended his range of currency to include silver and bronze, as well as gold issues. He was one of the first Britannic kings to mint coins inscribed with his name. He was the grandfather of Caratacus and Togodumnus and a contemporary of Addedomaros of the Trinovantes. He ruled over the lands north of the Thames in a kingdom equivalent to the counties of Hertfordshire and Middlesex. (Numisantica – http://www.numisantica.com/Wikimedia Commons/CC-BY-SA-3.0)

Verica appears to have been a successful ruler for some 30 years until his reign ended around AD 40, when his kingdom was striven by internal strife and subsequently overrun by the Catuvellauni, a tribe that was then being aggressively expansive under its similarly long-lived and successful ruler Cunobelinus (Shakespeare's Cymbeline). He was the blood or adopted son of Tasciovanus, and thus possibly a descendant of Cassivellaunus, the opponent of Iulius Caesar. Cunobelinus had united the territories of the Trinovantes and the Catuvellauni to form the most powerful kingdom in Britannia for the three decades – no mean achievement – prior to the Claudian invasion. He ruled his kingdom from a new capital he had conquered at Camulodunum–Colchester, which brought him into economic and political contact with Rome via Gaul.

Driven from his kingdom during the course of a 'civil war', Verica (or Βέρικος, as Cassius Dio calls him) fled across the Oceanus and 'persuaded Claudius to send a force there' (60.19.1); the emperor, who had only just been thrust into power, now had a 'legitimate' reason to invade Britannia. On numerous occasions in our own times, foreign military force can be used to prop up or restore 'rightful' leaders – however we choose to define that word. Nevertheless, as *rex*, Verica was nominally a friend and ally of Rome, and, besides, the Atrebates under his long rule appear to have had open trade and diplomatic links with the empire.

Cunobelinus had three living sons that we know of. Togodumnus, the eldest, succeeded his powerful father sometime before the Claudian invasion. Caratacus, the second son, already showing signs of being a capable and resourceful leader, began to carve out a kingdom for himself south of the Thames in the territory of the Atrebates. It is possible to see signs of the extent of his influence from the evidence of coins bearing his image. It appears he also at this time began to forge useful alliances with his southern and western neighbours.

It is the third son, however, that concerns us at this juncture. He was Adminius (or Amminus, as he should strictly be called), a deeply bitter and disappointed man, mainly because he had not been included in what he saw as a fair share out of his father's dominions. When the political situation shifted in south-eastern Britannia, Adminius switched to Rome and made an appeal to Caius Caligula for help against his two brothers (Suet. *Calig.* 44.2). It was this appeal, while not acted on at once, which was followed by another to his successor, Claudius, by Verica. Of course, the irony here is the fact that Verica had been driven to do so by Caratacus' invasion of his kingdom.

CHRONOLOGY

c. 320 BC	Pytheas, a Massiliote navigator, explores the Atlantic and the North Sea.
55 BC	Iulius Caesar crosses to Britannia from his base in Gaul.
54 BC	Iulius Caesar returns to Britannia.
AD 37	Death of Tiberius and succession of Caius Caligula.
AD 40–42	Mauritanian rebellion – suppressed by Caius Suetonius Paulinus.
AD 40	Caius Caligula joins Rhineland legions – 'plans' to invade Britannia.
AD 41	Assassination of Caius Caligula – Praetorian Guard elevate his uncle, Claudius.
AD 42	Rebellion of Lucius Arruntius Camillus Scribonianus, *legatus pro praetore* of Dalmatia.
AD 43	Claudian invasion with four legions under Aulus Plautius.
	Battles of the Medway and the Thames – death of Togodumnus and defeat of Caratacus.
	Arrival of Claudius – capture of Camulodunum–Colchester.
AD 43–44	Campaigns west (Legio II Augusta under Vespasianus), Midlands (*Legiones* XX and XIIII Gemina) and east (Legio VIIII Hispana).
AD 44	Triumph of Claudius in Rome – names his son Britannicus.
AD 48	Publius Ostorius Scapula, second governor of Britannia, suppresses Iceni.
AD 49	Ostorius Scapula transfers Legio XX from Camulodunum–Colchester to Glevum–Gloucester (Kingsholm).
AD 50	Foundation of *colonia* at Camulodunum–Colchester.
AD 51	Ostorius Scapula defeats Caratacus; Silures (and others) continue to resist.
AD 52	Death of Ostorius Scapula – Aulus Didius Gallus becomes governor.
AD 54	Death of Claudius – succession of Nero.
AD 60	Caius Suetonius Paulinus, fifth governor of Britannia, attacks Mona–Anglesey.
AD 60–61	Uprising of Iceni under Boudica – suppressed by Suetonius Paulinus.

OPPOSING COMMANDERS

AULUS PLAUTIUS SILVANUS

Aulus Plautius Silvanus was a solid career man, a loyal and industrious servant of the Iulio-Claudian regime – links between his family and the ruling dynasty extended back to at least Livia. It is without doubt that the prime quality Claudius was looking for in the soon-to-be commander of the largest army within the empire was a steadfast loyalty to its commander-in-chief. Autocrats exist in a perpetual state of paranoia that their grip on power is under threat, and the emperor was rightly afraid of those who had large provincial armies at their disposal. As a long-standing friend of the Iulio-Claudians, by selecting Aulus Plautius, Claudius was putting the command of the invasion force into a safe pair of hands.

Aulus Plautius had served as the *legatus pro praetore* of Pannonia before his appointment to head the invasion of Britannia, and it was while he was in this post that he played a vital role in ensuring the continuing loyalty of the legions along the Danuvius (Danube). In the previous year – AD 42 – Lucius Arruntius Camillus Scribonianus (*cos.* AD 32), *legatus pro praetore* of Dalmatia and a descendant of Pompeius Magnus, attempted to raise a rebellion against Claudius; 'it was smothered in less than five days' (Suet. *Claud*. 13.2).

Aulus Plautius was to earn the rare tribute of a triumphal ovation on his eventual return to Rome for his part in the successful direction of operations during the invasion, and for laying the foundations upon which the province of Britannia would be constructed. Claudius even went out to meet the returning hero as he entered Rome, and was to show him other extraordinary signs of favour (Suet. *Claud*. 24.3).

TOGODUMNUS AND CARATACUS

Cunobelinus of the Catuvellauni was the most famous of the Britannic kings of the period. He was powerful enough to be called by Suetonius *rex Britannorum*, 'king of the Britons' (*Calig*. 44.2), though his coinage indicates that he controlled what we call Hertfordshire, Essex and parts of Kent. However, we know from Cassius Dio that by the time of the Claudian invasion, the king was dead, and had been succeeded by his two violently anti-Roman sons, Togodumnus and Caratacus. Of the two, Caratacus is the only one whose existence is verified by Catuvellaunian coinage marked with the letters CARA, though the two brothers first appear in the invasion account of Cassius Dio.

Togodumnus was to either fall sometime after the Medway battle, or succumb to wounds inflicted upon him. His brother, however, was to resist the Romans for a further eight years as a guerrilla leader. During this time, Caratacus was to lead the occupiers a merry dance until the Celtic equivalent of Fortuna decided to desert him. He was betrayed by Cartimandua, queen of the client kingdom, the Brigantes, fettered and promptly handed over to the Roman authorities (Tac. *Hist.* 3.45.1, cf. *Ann.* 12.36.1). Subsequently, he was dispatched to Claudius in Rome.

If Caratacus possessed the outstanding military skills that are attributed to him by Tacitus, then he must have developed and acquired them through hard and bitter experience after the campaigning season of AD 43. As Tacitus was to point out, Caratacus' 'deficiency in strength [viz. numbers] was compensated by superior cunning and topographical knowledge' (*Ann.* 12.33). At the Medway, there were certainly no overt displays of such skills by Caratacus, for, as Cassius Dio makes abundantly clear, 'the barbarians thought the Romans would be unable to cross without a bridge; in consequence they had camped in careless fashion on the far bank' (60.20.2).

LEGIONARY LEGATES

The legion's commanding officer was a *legatus Augusti legionis*, appointed from the senatorial order by the emperor to command in his name, and by the end of the Iulio-Claudian era, only a senator who had already held the praetorship at Rome was eligible. The command of a legion in that case had a definite place in the hierarchy of the senatorial order, and was usually held for a period of roughly three years. At a later stage in his career, once having held the consulship, a senator was eligible for a provincial governorship. Moreover, if the post was to be held in an armed province such as Britannia, the governor was ranked as a *legatus Augusti pro praetore* ('praetorian legate of Augustus') and would have assumed control over the legions stationed therein, which were four in the case of Britannia. Accordingly, the emperor commanded his army and governed his provinces through his *legati*, who held delegated power or *imperium*.

Titus Flavius Vespasianus
Titus Flavius Vespasianus (AD 9–79) was a senior senator of obscure Italian origin, 'baseborn' in the eyes of those that 'mattered'. Nonetheless, this represented a culmination of an important process, which brought an Italian into government, many Italians having come to prominence during Octavianus' devastating and bloody rise to power. Like the men closest to Octavianus, Vespasianus was not a member of the traditional Roman nobility; his family had run a banking business in the small Latium town of Rieti. His paternal grandfather, Titus Flavius Petro, became the first to rise above the common herd, gaining the rank of centurion and fighting at Pharsalus for Pompeius Magnus in 48 BC. Surviving the civil wars, he subsequently became a *publicanus*, a tax collector

(Suet. *Vesp.* 1.2) Vespasianus and his elder brother, Titus Flavius Sabinus – whom we will come to – were the first of the family to gain entrance to the Senate. Vespasianus was a sure-footed commander and a shrewd politician, though he obviously came across more as a tough old soldier of straightforward speech than anything else (one suspects that he was born a rough soldier and only made a canny politician).

The history of Vespasianus' rise is full of lessons. As a young officer of equestrian status, he had risen steadily through the military ranks, first serving as one of the five equestrian military tribunes, *tribuni militum angusticlavii*, in a legion engaged in mopping up unruly mountaineers in Thrace, and later as a *quaestor* in the joint province of Crete and Cyrenaica (Suet. *Vesp.* 2.3, Dio 59.12.3). He had been an *aedilis* and a *praetor* under Caius Caligula, and it was during his aedileship that he incurred the wrath of the madcap emperor, who was furious that the streets of Rome were filthy. As it was one of Vespasianus' duties as *aedilis* to keep the streets of the capital clean, the apoplectic emperor ordered some Praetorians to stuff his senatorial toga with ordure, which they did with gusto (Suet. *Vesp.* 5.3). Conceivably, the emperor viewed Vespasianus (undistinguished as yet) as somebody who had climbed too quickly above his station. It is conceivable, of course, that the emperor was a man with borderline antisocial personality disorder, a psychopath even, a man-child with no conscience and no empathy for anybody.

Marble portrait bust of Vespasianus (Museum of Archaeology, Thessaloniki, inv. 1055), which perfectly illustrates his heavy square jaw and bull neck. It is hard to imagine the frank and forceful Titus Flavius Vespasianus as an emperor. Vespasianus seemed, rather, to be a man born for the trials and tribulations of war, endowed with courage, endurance, willpower and unshakable determination. Only just in his mid-twenties, he was appointed to the command of Legio II Augusta by Claudius. (© Nic Fields)

Fortunately for him, Vespasianus had been well liked by Claudius, who would even grant him the trappings of a triumph, *ornamenta triumphalia*, for his part in the invasion of southern Britannia as the *legatus legionis* of Legio II Augusta. According to Flavius Josephus, 'by force of arms he had added Britannia, till then unknown, to the empire, so enabling Nero's father Claudius, who had not lifted a finger himself, to celebrate a triumph' (*B Iud.* 3.1.2 [3]). Here, Josephus deliberately plays up the role of Vespasianus in Britannia, which is an obvious flattering exaggeration (after all, the author owed him his life), since he had commanded only one of the four legions that had made up the invasion army. Even so, during the campaign Vespasianus had stood well with II Augusta, both as a soldier and as a man, and in Tacitus' estimation he was a model commander 'scarcely different from a common soldier in his appearance and dress' (*Hist.* 2.5.1).

In short, Vespasianus was a plain, candid man who had kept a local Italian accent. Like the elderly Tiberius before him, he was a proven soldier with experience of the provinces both east and west. Yet he had none of

Coloured reconstruction of the funerary stele (Grosvenor Museum, Chester) of Caecilius Avitus from Emerita Augusta (Merida, Spain), *optio* of Legio XX, depicting him holding his *hastile*, staff of office. The original stele is post-AD 61 because it was from the victory over the Boudican rebels that the legion was awarded by Nero its honorific titles Valeria Victrix, 'Powerful and Victorious'. The importance of these tombstones is that they give the full name, rank and unit of the soldier, his age and years of service and his detailed effigy in undress uniform. They were also painted. The legion was last recorded in Britannia towards the end of the 3rd century AD, when it was based at Deva–Chester. (Wolfgang Sauber/Wikimedia Commons/CC-BY-SA-3.0)

Tiberius' touchiness or patrician pride, and even his imperial portrait busts show a plain 'Italian' style of realism, not the classicizing ideal look of Augustus or Nero. His chief fault – no great weight in the balance – was his tightfistedness.

Titus Flavius Sabinus

It was universally agreed that before Vespasianus became emperor, the dignity of the Flavians centred on his elder brother, Titus Flavius Sabinus (d. AD 69). A sentence in Cassius Dio has been interpreted to mean that Sabinus came to Britannia as a ὑποστρατηγοῦντα, 'staff officer' (60.20.3), to his brother, which given his seniority seems rather odd. Cassius Dio was more of a compiler than a historian, and he tended to accept his material without any critical appraisal. Moreover, his monumental 80-book history of Rome, which is an amalgam of Greek and Roman elements written in antiquated Attic Greek, is difficult and corrupt, not to mention the author's own remoteness from the events of the invasion by some 150 years. But our leading authority of the Claudian invasion is Cassius Dio (60.19–20), and it is difficult to make into a coherent narrative without stretching the meaning and employing a bit of imagination, all of which would not be necessary if we had the lost sections of Tacitus' *Annales*.

To return to that ambiguous sentence of Cassius Dio: It has been demonstrated by one classical scholar that with a minor emendation, we can infer Sabinus was not a staff officer under his younger brother, but actually a ὑποστρατηγος, the Greek term for a *legatus legionis*, legionary legate. However, a legate to which one of the other three legions (VIIII Hispana, XIIII Gemina, or XX), if this supposition is indeed correct, we have no means of knowing.

After campaigning in Britannia, Sabinus would go on to govern Moesia for seven years (AD 49–56), was *praefectus urbi* (city prefect) twice under Nero (AD 56–60, AD 62–68), and once again from Otho's succession onwards. During the seven years he had governed Moesia, and the 12 years he had served as *praefectus urbi*, the only charge ever brought against him was his passion for long-windedness. After a successful public career extending over 35 years, his life was to come to a tragic, bloody end. When the Vitellian forces captured Rome during that dreadful year of anarchy (AD 69), Sabinus was heavily manacled and dragged before Vitellius, whose slender authority was unable to save him. In the spirit of unsparing hatred and savage inhumanity, the *praefectus urbi* was butchered and mutilated by the Vitellian soldiers (Tac. *Hist.* 3.74.2).

Cnaeus Hosidius Geta

The family of the Hosidii hailed from Histonium (Vasto, Abruzzo), a small town on the Adriatic coast of Picenum. Cnaeus Hosidius Geta is perhaps the subject of a fragmentary inscription (*ILS* 971) from Histonium, which refers to a legionary legate taking part in the Claudian invasion of Britannia and consequently being awarded *ornamenta triumphalia*.

Cnaeus Hosidius Geta is presumably the same commander who had recently performed with distinction in Mauretania. On becoming emperor, Claudius had inherited the war in this client kingdom, which had been caused by his predecessor, Caius Caligula. It was sometime after the spring of AD 40 when Caligula had ordered the arrest and execution of its king, Ptolemaios (r. AD 20–40), grandson of Marcus Antonius and Kleopatra VII, 'king, ally and friend of the Roman people', and then incorporated his kingdom into the empire (Dio 59.25.1). The rebellion had been raised by the freedman Aedemon, a former household slave of Ptolemaios, who out of loyalty to his murdered king wanted revenge.

It was in the year prior to the Claudian invasion – AD 42 – that Hosidius Geta, commanding a legion, was part of the punitive campaigns into Mauretania headed by Caius Suetonius Paulinus, the same commander who would later crush the Boudican rebellion. Though Aedemon's rebellion was none too successful, a number of Mauri chiefs took the opportunity to raise their tribes against Rome in a quest for their lost liberty. Hosidius Geta defeated Sabalus, one such Mauri chief, twice, and after gathering as much water as could be carried, pursued him into the desert. Cassius Dio continues the story:

Funerary stele (Mittelrheinisches Landesmuseum, Mainz) of Cnaeus Musius, aquilifer of Legio XIIII Gemina. He wears a harness displaying his military decorations, a couple of torques and a set of nine *phalerae*. The stele is pre-Claudian invasion, as Musius was buried in Mogontiacum–Mainz. Note also, the legion only bears the honorific title Gemina. The inscription (*CIL* xiii.6901) reads: CN(aeus) MVSIVS T(iti) F(ilius) / GAL(eria) VELEIAS AN(norum) / XXXII STIP(endiorum) XV / AQVILIF(er) LEG(ionis) XIIII GEM(inae) / M(arcus) MVSIVS / (centurio) FRATER POSVIT. Musius signed up when he was just 17 years of age, served 15 years, during which time he saw action (probably during the Tiberian campaigns in Germania), and was buried by his brother Marcus, a centurion, probably in the same legion. (Carole Raddato/Wikimedia Commons/CC-BY-SA-2.0)

But when this [water] began to give out and was no more to be had, he found himself in the direst straits. For the barbarians, on their part, could hold out a long time anyway against thirst as a result of habit, and moreover could always get at least some water by familiarity with the country, and so they managed to get along; whereas the Romans, for the opposite reasons, found it impossible to advance and difficult even to retreat. While Geta, then, was in a quandary as to what he should do, one of the natives who were at peace with the invaders persuaded him to try some incantations and enchantments, telling him that as the result of such rites abundant water had often been given to his people. No sooner had Geta followed this advice than so much rain fell from the sky as to allay the soldiers' thirst completely and at the same time alarm the enemy, who thought that heaven was coming to the assistance of the Roman general. (Dio 60.9.4–5)

Sabalus, having witnessed this 'miracle', believed Hosidius Geta possessed supernatural powers and promptly surrendered. As a result, the Roman legate and his sun-scorched soldiers were spared further hardships and the 'small desert war' ended. Sabalus' fate afterwards is unknown.

Then came the Claudian invasion. Hosidius Geta would be *consul suffectus* with his fellow Britannia campaigner Titus Sabinus Flavius in AD 47.

OPPOSING FORCES

The Roman army of the early principate was a professional force of legionaries, auxiliaries and fleet personnel who had enlisted for extended periods, and who regarded the army or navy as a definite career. Enlistment was not for the duration of a particular conflict, but for 25 years (26 in the navy), and men were sometimes retained even longer. The loyalty of the army (and navy) was to the emperor, as commander-in-chief, and not to the Senate or the people of Rome.

As an instrument of war, the army of the early principate presented a powerful picture, and there is certainly little about it that a modern infantry soldier would fail to recognize. It comprised a professional standing force of a modern size that did not rely on conscription, and where military training, institutionalized discipline, arms factories, administrative and combat staffs, military maps, roads, logistics systems, military hospitals, intelligence services, communications, strategy and tactics, rank structures, scheduled promotions, military decorations, permanent records, personnel files, state-issued uniforms, regular pay and even military pension schemes – to name but a few – had already become part of everyday, military life.

The opposite is true of Iron Age Celtic armies. These tended to be fragile, virtually clouds of individuals, almost as much in competition with each other for the displaying of valour and the winning of prestige as in conflict with the foe. They consequently lacked cohesion and staying power: If one part of the army wavered, alarm could spread with terrific speed. However, the Celts saw warfare as an intrinsic extension of their culture. As a consequence, warfare in Britannia before the arrival of the Romans was essentially a matter of tribal feuding and cross-border raiding, combined with the lifting of livestock and people – the warring values of tribal life being based on a cattle bargain and the capturing of slaves being a natural part of perennial tribal conflict.

The legendary tale from early Irish literature *Táin Bó Cúailnge* (*The Cattle Raid of Cooley*) gives us a glimpse of this pre-Roman Iron Age world: '"Men are slain, women stolen, cattle lifted, ye men of Ulster!" cried Sualtaim [the human father of Cúchulainn]' (chapter 24). Although first written down at the turn of the 12th century, the *Táin Bó Cúailnge* is set in the 1st century AD, and it is received wisdom that it contains a genuine memory of Iron Age Celtic warfare, and the warfare it describes is the business of small armed bands. Iron Age Celtic societies, as a consequence, were far less militaristic than the Roman contemporary that was to triumph over them, in the sense that their agriculturally based, unurbanized and undeveloped nature made them incapable of raising, supplying and organizing proper armies, and left them to evolve a style of raiding, of hit-and-run tactics, to be used in cattle raids and the like rather than full-scale warfare. Having said all that, it should be recognized that the Britons did offer stiff resistance to Iulius Caesar during his two summer visits, and to the Claudian invasion of AD 43.

ROMAN

The Roman navy

Rome was not a natural sea power in the way the Greek states, the Hellenistic kingdoms and Carthage had been, and this is reflected in the Roman attitude to naval warfare, which sought to capitalize on the discipline and clout of their soldiery at sea. Thus, boarding and entering with marines was the principal means of overcoming their nautical enemies. However, the day of major fleet actions in the Mediterranean was over. The entire Mediterranean littoral, with all its harbours, was Roman, and despite the occasional outbreak, piracy had long been reduced to a comparatively insignificant problem. The observation of Philo Iudaeos, writing during the reign of Caius Caligula, is especially valuable: '[Augustus] is the man who swept the seas of pirate skiffs and filled it with commerce' (*Leg.* 146).

Despite the operational seascape having changed, however, the formation of a permanent navy was one of the preoccupations of the victor of Actium, Octavianus. As a result, there were two main fleets – the Classis Ravennas based at the head of the Adriatic at Ravenna, and the Classis Misenensis based on the Tyrrhenian at Misenum (Miseno) equidistant from Sicily, Sardinia and Corsica – and a permanent squadron at Forum Iulii (Fréjus) east of Massilia (Marseille) on the coast of Gallia Narbonensis (Suet. *Aug.* 49.1, Tac. *Ann.* 4.5, *CIL* xii.257, cf. Veg. *Mil.* 4.31). From the reign of Claudius onwards, the Classis Misenensis had a detachment stationed at Ostia, a port especially important for the reception and storage of the grain imported from overseas and destined for Rome. In fact, it was from Ostia that Claudius and his entourage sailed to be present at the finale of the invasion of Britannia (Suet. *Claud.* 17.2, Dio 60.21.3).

The ponderous polyremes, super ships which no modern shipyard would care to try and construct, had disappeared. These had been the top war vessels of the Hellenistic kingdoms, but history in the long run has justified the states that adhered to moderate-sized warships. An estimation of the composition of the two main fleets can be made with confidence. Epigraphical evidence records a *hexeres*, 'six', the *Ops* (named after the goddess of abundance), at Misenum (*CIL* vi.3163, x.3560, x.3611, xiv.232), and one or two quinqueremes in both the fleets, but otherwise they appear to have consisted of a limited number of quadriremes and small, swift *liburnae*, but mostly of triremes. Since 'sixes' (and 'sevens') were traditionally used by the Romans as

Funerary stele (Musée archéologique, Strasbourg, inv. 2431) of Caius Largennius, a soldier of Legio II Augusta, found in the Strasbourg district of Koenigshoffen (1878). The inscription (*CIL* xiii.5978) reads: C(aius) LARGENNIVS / C(aii filius) FAB(ia) LVC(a) MIL(es)/ LEG(ionis) II (centuria) SCAEVAE / AN(norum) XXXVII STIP(endiorum) / XVIII H(ic) S(itus) E(st). Caius was born in Luca, (Lucca, Italy), was of the Fabia voting-tribe, and stationed in Argentoratum–Strasbourg, dying at the age of 37 after 18 years of service. As he was evidently buried in Argentoratum, it is plain that he died before his legion departed the Rhine frontier for the invasion of Britannia. (Ji-Elle/Wikimedia Commons/CC-BY-SA-3.0)

flagships and viewed by them as being exceptionally large, the dividing line between smaller (*minoris formae*) and larger (*maioris formae*) warships seems to occur, as Livy (34.26.11, 37.23.4–5) indicates, between 'threes' and 'fours'. The main fleets, therefore, were equipped mainly for tasks that required speed and agility, rather than full-blown naval engagements that involved prow-to-prow ramming attacks.

Such operational tasks included the transport of emperors and governors, escort duty for the vital grain shipment to Rome and for army expeditions, such as the Claudian invasion of Britannia, and from time to time pursuing the occasional pirate. We should abandon the misconceived notion of naval patrolling, namely, staying at sea on watch for other vessels, which is in fact an anachronism for the ancient Mediterranean and not mentioned in our literary sources. Similarly, the Claudian invasion was not a question of naval or combined-arms strategy, but consisted of no more than carrying an unopposed expeditionary force in transports and warships across what we know as the Strait of Dover.

A 1/10-scale model reconstruction of a Roman quadrireme (Museum für Antike Schiffahrt, Mainz), based on a 1st-century BC/1st-century AD graffito sketch of a warship found in Chiesa di San Pietro, Alba Fucens, Italy. The graffito is inscribed *navis tetreris longa*, which designates it as a 'four', viz. two levels of oars and double-manned. Classed as *maioris formae*, a major ship, by the Romans, the quadrireme was valued for its speed and manoeuvrability, while its relatively shallow draught made it ideal for coastal operations. Reconstruction indicates a likely displacement of about 60 tonnes, but a capacity to carry about 75 marines, making the 'four' into an economical yet well-armed ship. (Carole Raddato/ Wikimedia Commons/ CC-BY-SA-2.0)

Naval organization

The Romans marched on their feet and conquered by land. Accordingly, the relative unimportance of the two main fleets in the greater scheme of things is indicated by the status of their personnel and commanders. Ordinary seamen were normally not citizens, but *peregrini*, freeborn inhabitants of the empire without Roman or Latin rights, like the soldiers of the *auxilia*. Indeed, we find few of Italian origin; most of the seamen appear to have originated from the seafaring peoples of the eastern Mediterranean (Starr 1975 [1941], Table I). Naval personnel signed up for 26 years, a year longer than auxiliaries, receiving Roman citizenship upon *honesta missio*, honourable discharge (*CIL* xvi.1, xvi.66).

A ship's complement, regardless of its size, was organized as a *centuria* under its *centurio* (*classicus*). Epigraphic evidence shows that seamen, regardless of their function, called themselves *milites*, soldiers, rather than *nautae*, seamen, and no distinction appears to have been made between oarsmen and marines as there had been in Greek and Hellenistic navies. Despite popular perceptions, the Roman navy relied on oarsmen of free status, and not on galley slaves.[3]

There were specialists and officer ranks, earning one-and-a-half times the base pay (*sesquipliciarii*) or double the base pay (*dupliciarii*): doctors (*medici*), armourers (*armorum custodes*), musicians (*cornicines*, *tubicines*, *bucinatores*), principales or junior officers (*tessararii*, *suboptiones*, *optiones*),

---

3 In 37 BC, Octavianus did enrol 20,000 slaves in his own fleet, in preparation for war with Sextus Pompeius, but freed them before formally enlisting them (Suet. *Aug.* 16.1).

standard-bearers (*signiferi*, *vexillarii*), and secretarial and headquarter types (*adiutores*, *scribae*, *librarii*, *beneficiarii*). Alongside these were specialist ranks derived from Greek and Hellenistic navies, who were concerned with the rowing and sailing of the ship. There were the craftsmen (*fabri*), the sail-trimmers (*velarii*), the supply officers (*nauphylaces*), the rowing masters (*celeustae* or *pausarii*), the bow-officer (*proretae*) and the helmsmen (*gubernatores*).

Individual ships of all types were under the command of a *trierarchus*, and squadrons were under a *nauarchus*, the highest-ranking one bearing the title *nauarchus princeps*. All of these naval commanders were of a rank equivalent to an auxiliary centurion. Such men would normally have started out as seamen, and would have come up through the ranks. There would therefore have been considerable professionalism throughout the navy.

Fleet commanders, on the other hand, were high-ranking equestrians, that is, non-senatorial, although a couple of freedmen are known to have been appointed to these posts under Claudius. They bore the title of *praefectus classis*, and in our period of study ranked just above the *praefecti* of auxiliary units, from whose number they had been promoted (viz. *praefectus cohortis* > *tribunus militum angusticlavius* > *praefectus equitum*). They were assisted by a *subpraefectus* of similar background, though this rank is not attested until the reign of Nero.

Provincial fleets

The Classis Misenensis was the largest fleet: It has been calculated that, in the time of Claudius, its manpower strength exceeded 10,000. The Classis Ravennas was perhaps half as large. At the same time, smaller provincial fleets were raised to meet the needs of local conditions. In the eastern Mediterranean there was the Classis Alexandrina, based in the great harbour of Alexandria. At the other end of the empire there was the Classis Germanica, established in 12 BC under Drusus (Dio 54.32.2), and the one that concerns us here, the Classis Britannica, first attested in AD 43, perhaps at Gesoriacum–Boulogne-sur-Mer. Three years earlier – AD 40 – Caius Caligula had made preparations for an invasion of Britannia, which included collecting what transports (*naves onerariae*) and warships (*naves longae*), including triremes, he could, and building others. The bulk of this fleet is likely to have remained at Gesoriacum–Boulogne-sur-Mer, if this was the location, to form the core of the fleet used by Aulus Plautius for the successful invasion three years later.

The Claudian invasion would require massive naval preparations, as Caesar was quick to appreciate during the planning stage of his second invasion. John Peddie (1987, pp. 37–41) has estimated that the Claudian invasion force needed at least 933, if not around 1,000, vessels to carry it across to Britannia, a fleet comparable to that which carried Caesar on his second invasion. This, he says, numbered 'over 800 ships' (*B Gall.* 5.8.6).

The Claudian fleet in turn became the permanent Classis Britannica, consisting of *liburnae* and at least one trireme (*CIL* xiii.3564, Tac. *Agr.* 28.1). It was based initially at Rutupiae–Richborough in the shelter of the Wantsum Channel, a stretch of tidal water that separated the Isle of Thanet (Tanatus Insula) from the rest of Kent. And lest we forget, it is important to

Funerary stele (Yorkshire Museum, York, inv. 1998.19) of Lucius Duccius Rufinus, a *signifer* of Legio VIIII Hispana, found on the site of Holy Trinity Priory, York (1688). The inscription (*RIB* 673) reads: L(ucius) DVCCIVS / L(uci) (filius) VOLT(inia) (tribu) RVFI/NVS VIEN(na) / SIGNIF(er) LEG(ionis) VIIII / AN(norum) XXIIXX / H(ic) S(itus) E(st). Lucius was born in Vienna (Vienne, France), was of the Voltinia voting-tribe, died at the age of 28 and was buried in Eboracum–York, where he had been based since AD 71. A mystery has surrounded the disappearance of this legion from Britannia, and a great Roman defeat has been visualized, leading to its replacement by Legio VI Victrix Pia Fidelis. However, the discovery of traces of this unit on the lower Rhine opens up other possibilities. (Carole Raddato/Wikimedia Commons/ CC-BY-SA-2.0)

(Above) Blade and tang of a *gladius* (Musée d'archéologie nationale, Saint-Germain-en-Laye, inv. 49824) found at Trévoux, département du l'Ain. It has a total length of 610mm, the strong, broad blade itself measuring 479mm. It belongs to the first of two models of *gladius*, the 'Mainz/Fulham' type with its long, efficient stabbing point. The *gladius* was a highly manoeuvrable and efficient close-quarters weapon, a true infantryman's weapon, nicely balanced and useful for either cutting or thrusting. (Below) Replica of the *gladius* (Archaeological Museum Carnuntum, Bad Deutsch-Altenburg), known as the Sword of Tiberius; it was discovered in 1848 outside Mainz, the site of a legionary fortress. At the top of the tinned and gilded bronze scabbard is a figurative scene in which, it is argued, Tiberius is shown, enthroned and receiving his adopted son Germanicus in AD 17, the victorious commander of the Rhineland army (also the father of Caius Caligula and brother of Claudius, both future emperors). To the left and right of Tiberius are the goddess Victory and the god Mars (probably), respectively. (Above, © Esther Carré; below, MatthiasKabel/Wikimedia Commons/CC-BY-SA-3.0)

remember that there is no literary reference to the Classis Britannica by that name, although tiles stamped 'CLBR' are common along the east Kent coast, especially at Lemanis–Lympne, and in London.

The Roman army

In war, Rome had no secret weapon, and the basis of its world domination was forged from an indomitable blend of unlimited manpower, military skill and might, relentless aggression, doggedness in adversity and moral superiority, all of which was occasionally compounded with a large dose of self-deception and a long streak of cruelty. Its wars had always been fought with a pitiless dedication to total victory. Yet Rome's world dominion rested on its military arm, whose strength and length were definite. The Roman army, which relied on heavily equipped infantry, was best suited for high-intensity warfare against a dense agricultural population with conquerable assets. It was less well suitable for mobile warfare against lightly equipped opponents. Rome would settle for what its army could handle and its agriculturists could exploit, and thus excluded the steppe, the alpine, the forest and the desert.

A career for life

The army itself seems to have been most attractive as a fixed career to the poorest citizens. For such men, the legions offered a roof over their heads, food in their bellies and a regular income in coin. No surprises there. Basic military pay was not the road to riches, but there was always the chance of bounties and emoluments, and the certainty of a discharge bonus. Overall, a soldier's life was more secure than that of an itinerant labourer, and he enjoyed a superior status too. Of course, we must remember the harsher

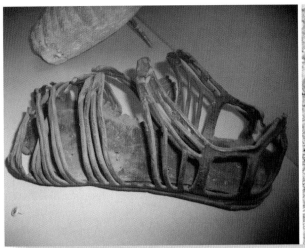

side of such a career. A soldier, who must be in the thick of things, ran the risk of being killed or crippled by battle or disease, but also on an everyday basis was subject to the army's brutal discipline. Most of us are familiar with the centurion 'Give-me-Another', *cedo alteram*, so called because of his habit of beating a soldier's back until his gnarled vine-stick (*vitis*) snapped, and then shouting for a second and a third (Tac. *Ann.* 1.23.1). Yet to many people in the empire who pulled through at subsistence level, the well-fed soldier with his ordered existence in his well-built and clean camp must have seemed comfortably off. So the legions became permanent units with their own numbers and titles, and many were to remain in existence for centuries to come – and XIIII Gemina, one of the Claudian invasion legions, may be taken as a specimen of them all.

The legion was raised by Iulius Caesar, being initially deployed in the spring of 57 BC, during the war in Gaul, just prior to his punitive campaign against the Belgae of north-east Gaul. Caesar implies the existence of a Legio XIIII in his account of the battle against the Nervii in the late summer of that year (Caes. *B Gall.* 2.8, 2.19, 2.26). Three-and-a-half years later, this unit was all but annihilated by the Belgic Eburones, led by their chief Ambiorix, in the first weeks of 53 BC (ibid. 5.37). It was immediately reconstituted, and the soldiers of the new legion probably earned their spurs during the long and arduous siege of Alesia in 52 BC.

The title Gemina implies one legion made from two, probably by Octavianus after Actium. It was stationed in Mogontiacum–Mainz from AD 9 until AD 43. After the first phase of the Claudian invasion and occupation, XIIII Gemina was stationed in Ratae Corieltauvorum–Leicester, perhaps sharing the base with VIIII Hispana. Under the *propraetor* Publius Ostorius Scapula (AD 47–52), the legion was sent against the Cornovii in the west, and later against the Deceangi, a tribe in what is now northern Wales. Another victim was the tribe of the Brigantes in the north. The legion was redeployed at Lindum–Lincoln soon after (*RIB* 249). In the following decade, Legio XIIII Gemina fought against tribes in today's Wales: the Silures, the Ordovices and once again the Deceangi. After AD 55, it was based at Viroconium Cornoviorum–Wroxeter, the tribal centre of the Cornovii on the east bank of the Severn, where it was to remain for some time (*RIB* 292, 294, 296).

When the Iceni queen Boudica rose in revolt in AD 60, Legio XIIII Gemina played a crucial part in her eventual defeat (Tac. *Ann.* 14.34–7), being awarded as a consequence the honorific title Martia Victrix (victorious, blessed by Mars) – first attested in AD 66 (*ILS* 2648). It was to leave Britannia in AD 66, in preparation for a leading role in Nero's projected Caspian campaigns, to be temporarily returned around AD 70, before leaving permanently soon after (Tac. *Hist.* 4.68).

The legions

Legions were probably in the order of 5,000-men strong (all ranks) and composed of Roman citizens, for citizenship was a qualification for entry into a legion. Legionaries were mostly volunteers, drawn initially from Italy (especially the north), but increasingly from the provinces. As the 1st century AD progressed, many recruits in the west were coming from the Iberian provinces, Gallia Narbonensis and Noricum, and in the east from the Greek cities of Macedonia and Asia Minor. Thus, by the end of the century, the number of Italians serving in the legions was small. Statistics based on nomenclature and the origins of individuals show that of all the legionaries serving in the period from Augustus to Caligula, some 65 per cent were Italians, while in the period from Claudius to Nero this figure was 48.7 per cent, dropping even further to 21.4 per cent in the period from Vespasianus to Trajan. Thereafter, the contribution of Italians to the manpower of the legions was negligible, individual volunteers preferring service in the more prestigious and much more lucrative Praetorian Guard (Webster 1979, p. 108). It must be emphasized, however, that these statistics represent all legionaries in the empire. In reality, there was a dichotomy in recruitment patterns between the western and eastern provinces, with legions in the west drawing upon Gaul, Iberia and northern Italy, while those stationed in the east very quickly harnessed the local resources of manpower.

Legions consisted of ten cohorts (*cohortes*), with six centuries (*centuriae*) of 80 men in each cohort – after our period of study, from AD 70 or thereabouts, the first cohort (*cohors prima*), the most senior, would be of double strength, that is five centuries of 160 hand-picked men. Commanded by a centurion (*centurio*) and his second-in-command (*optio*), a standard century (*centuria*) was divided into ten eight-man subunits (*contubernia*), each *contubernium* sharing a tent on campaign and pair of rooms in a barrack block, eating, sleeping and fighting together. Much like small tactical units in today's professional armies, this state of affairs tended to foster a tight bond between 'messmates' (*contubernales*). Male bonding would explain why many soldiers (*milites*) preferred to serve their entire military career in the ranks despite the opportunities for secondment as *beneficiarii* to specialized tasks or for promotion within their own unit. Nonetheless, a soldier (*miles*) who performed a special function was excused heavy fatigues, which made

(Left) Roman *pilum* (Gunzenhausen Archäologisches Museum). (Right) Reconstruction of a Roman *pilum* (National Roman Legion Museum, Caerleon-Isca Silurum). Legionaries were equipped with two of these, which they hurled before drawing their swords. Instead of having the whole business-end tempered, the tempering was confined to the elongated pyramidal iron head. This ensured that the long, thin iron-shank remained quite soft, and was liable to buckle and bend under the weight of the wooden shaft when the *pilum* fixed itself in a shield, armour or flesh. (Left, Wolfgang Sauber/Wikimedia Commons/CC-BY-SA-3.0; right, © Nic Fields)

him an *immunis*, although he did not receive any extra pay for his skill (*Digest* 50.6.7). Finally, there was a small force of 120 horsemen (*equites legionis*) recruited from among the legionaries themselves. These *equites* acted as messengers, escorts and scouts, and were allocated to specific centuries rather than belonging to a formation of their own. Thus, the inscription (*RIB* 481) on a funerary stele from Deva–Chester describes an *eques* of Legio II Adiutrix Pia Fidelis as belonging to the *centuria* of Petronius Fidus. Citizen cavalry had probably disappeared after Marius' reforms, and certainly was not in evidence in Caesar's legions. The first noticeable reference to the 120 horsemen of a legion comes from Flavius Josephus (*B Iud.* 3.4.2 [68]), though the *equites* seem to have been revived as part of the Augustan army reforms.

The legion's commanding officer was a legate, *legatus Augusti legionis*, a subject we have already dealt with earlier. The other senior officers of the legion were six tribunes – one was a senator designate (*tribunus laticlavius*), and the other five were equestrians (*tribuni angusticlavii*) – and 60 centurions of graded seniority. In the hierarchy of command the senatorial tribune always ranked next to the legate, by virtue of his noble birth. His was a one-year post held before the age of 25 and prior to his entering the Senate as a *quaestor*. Such men were gaining first-hand experience in readiness for commanding their own legion in a few years' time. Their role was largely advisory.

Next in order of seniority came not the remaining five tribunes, but the *praefectus castrorum* (prefect of the camp), a post that required considerable and detailed knowledge of the legion, its personnel and the daily rounds of duties. As the name implies, the *praefectus castrorum* had general charge of the encampment or base. In addition, he saw to the maintenance of artillery, the medical services and military hospital, and supervised weapons training. Obviously, this senior officer provided a degree of professionalism and continuity, which the two senatorial officers might seem to lack.

Modern re-enactor equipped as a fully loaded legionary on display at Carnuntum 2008. Two of the scenes of Trajan's Column (First Dacian War, scenes 4/IV–5/V) depict the emperor's army crossing the Danuvius (Danube) on two parallel pontoon bridges, the legionaries marching with a wooden T-pole over their left shoulder carrying five objects: a netted bag for forage, a bronze cooking pot and *patera* for cooking and eating, a linen sack containing rations or spare clothing and a leather satchel probably for the retention of tools such as a saw, axe, sickle, chain and rope. (MatthiasKabel/Wikimedia Commons/CC-BY-SA-2.5)

(Inset, top left) Bronze *patera* (Museo Civico Archeologico, Bologna, inv. ROM 1334), dated to the 1st century AD. The Roman soldier may have been adorned with various pieces of killing hardware, but each also carried one of these, a humble mess tin, *patera*. (Main image) Reconstruction of a legionary satchel and *patera* made by a member of Legio XXI Rapax re-enactment group, on display at Sechseläuten 2011, Lindenhof 11 April 2011. (Inset, © Esther Carré; main image, Roland zh/Wikimedia Commons/ CC-BY-SA-3.0)

Haguenau/Coolus-type legionary helmet (Musée historique, Haguenau), found at Drusenheim and dated to the first half of the 1st century AD. Roman helmets, of Celtic inspiration, were made of iron or copper alloy (both bronze and brass are known). Bronze was a more expensive metal, but cheaper to work into a helmet; whereas iron helmets could only be beaten into shape, bronze ones were often 'spun' on a revolving former (a shaped piece of wood or stone) from annealed bronze sheet. Legionary helmets had been specifically designed to provide against cuts and blows from above the skull, to the face. The only weakness was at the back of the neck, where the horizontal projection stopped downward strokes, but not horizontal or upward sweeps. This bronze example is missing its cheek-guards. It bears a scratched inscription identifying its owner: (centuria) LVCC(i) VARRONIS, 'Varro of the century of Lucius'. (Pascal Radigue/Wikimedia Commons/ CC-BY-SA-3.0)

Immediately below the *praefectus castrorum* ranked the five equestrian tribunes. These tribunes held no independent command in the legion, but unlike the senatorial tribune they had already experienced leadership. This was in the capacity of a commander of an auxiliary infantry unit, and as a result they were each in a position to offer (if asked) their legate some practical advice on the handling and disposition of auxiliary forces in his command area. Equally, these men would have the chance to see a legion in action from within, which would stand them in good stead when (or if) they went on to further commands, such as a commander of an auxiliary cavalry unit.

The centurions in each cohort retained under the early principate the Republican titles: *pilus prior* and *pilus posterior*, *princeps prior* and *princeps posterior*, and *hastatus prior* and *hastatus posterior*. Within each cohort the order seniority among the centurions reflected their former positions in the old threefold battle lines of the manipular legion. The senior centurion of each cohort was the *pilus prior*, followed by the *princeps prior* and *hastatus prior*, then by the three *posterior* centurions in the same order. The senior centurions of the legion were those of the first cohort (*cohors prima*), with the *primus pilus* at their head, collectively known as the *primi ordines* ('front rankers'), and the junior ones those of the tenth cohort. Promotion thus consisted of a movement towards a lower-numbered cohort. The *primus pilus*, who commanded the first century of the first cohort and had charge of the eagle-standard (*aquila*), was the most senior centurion of the legion. He was an officer of considerable experience and influence, authorized to attend war councils, where the advice of this grizzled warrior was undoubtedly sought and greatly valued. He invariably went on to become the *praefectus castrorum*, his last post before retirement.

Detachments

The transfer of legions to different parts of the empire could leave long stretches of frontier virtually undefended, and wholesale transfers became unpopular as legions acquired local links. An extreme case must be that of Legio II Augusta. Reformed from an earlier legion by Augustus, namely II Sabina raised by the consul Vibius Pansa in 43 BC, II Augusta was part of the invasion army of AD 43; the legion was destined to be stationed in the province for the whole time Britannia was part of the empire.

Many recruits were the illegitimate sons of serving soldiers or veterans, that is, *origo castris* ('born in the camp' – e.g. *ILS* 2304). It is likely that most of them were illegitimate sons born to soldiers from local women living in the nearby *canabae legionis*, the extramural settlement associated with the garrison. Therefore, the custom developed of sending not an entire legion to deal with emergencies, but detachments drawn from the various legions of a province. Detachments from legions operating independently, or with other detachments, were known as *vexillationes*, named from the flag (*vexillum*) that identified them. Until the creation of field armies in the late principate,

(Left) Reconstruction of a legionary *scutum* (Jewry Wall Museum, Leicester), semi-cylindrical in shape, which afforded the legionary protection from the chin to the knees, and when held tightly to the body, covered half of it. Nevertheless, shields were expendable. Intended to deflect or absorb blows, shields would often have been damaged or destroyed in battle. Even so, *scuta* did not just have a defensive function in combat. (Right) Close view showing the heavy bronze *umbo* in detail. The large, centrally placed metallic boss projecting from the external face of a *scutum* made it a handy offensive weapon that could be used in a jabbing manner to drive back or punch opponents in close-quarter fighting. (© Nic Fields)

these *vexillationes* were the method of providing temporary reinforcements to frontier armies for major campaigns.

The auxiliaries

Under Augustus, the rather heterogeneous collection of auxiliary units (*auxilia*) serving Rome were completely reorganized as cohorts (*cohortes*) and 'wings' (*alae*), and given regular status within the new standing army. The reform itself can be associated with the advice allegedly given in 29 BC to Octavianus (as he was still known) by Maecenas, one of his closest confidants, that a standing army should be formed for the defence of the Roman empire 'drawn from the citizens, the subject nations, and the allies' (Dio 52.27.1). Whatever the truth of Maecenas' advice, the *auxilia* formed

(Left) Full-size manikin (Corinium Museum, Cirencester) of an auxiliary horseman. The manikin is wearing a Gallic-type mail shirt with shoulder cape. Note the *spatha*, a sword type based on the La Tène III sword, which hangs at the right hip. It required only one hand – vitally important when you are perched on the back of a horse – and surviving blades range from about 65 to 91.5cm in length with a width usually less than 4.4cm. Pommel, handgrip and guard were generally similar to *gladius* types. (Right) Auxiliary cavalry helmet (British Museum, London, inv. 1891, 1117.1) from Witcham Gravel, Ely, Cambridgeshire, dated *c.* AD 50–75. Only the decorative copper alloy casing remains; an iron core originally fitted under the casing. The cap, neck guard and cheek-guards were originally tinned. A characteristic feature of Roman cavalry helmets is the extension of the cheek-guards to cover the ears, commonly shaped as simulated ears. This example, however, has two raised ear protectors. (Left, © Nic Fields; right, Michael wal/ Wikimedia Commons/CC-BY-SA-3.0)

from the clients and allies of Rome were in existence before the death of Augustus in AD 14.

Trained to the same exacting standards of discipline as the legions, the men were long-service professionals, like the legionaries, and served in units that were equally permanent. Recruited from a wide range of warlike peoples who lived just within or on the periphery of Roman control, with Gauls, Thracians and Germans in heavy preponderance, the *auxilia* were freeborn non-citizens (*peregrini*), who, at least from the time of Claudius, received full Roman citizenship after 25 years of honourable service. This also included the grant of *conubium*, the right to formally marry women who were not citizens, which was to have far-reaching effects on the rapid spread of citizenship in the provinces.

Let us take as an example the funerary stele of Longinus Sdapeze, discovered in Colchester. In the form of a rider relief bearing an auxiliary horseman in action, he is pig-sticking a fallen enemy – a type of stele common to auxiliary troopers serving in the Germania and Britannia. This example is earliest in date, all of which belong to the 1st century AD:

LONGINVS SDAPEZE / MATYGI F(ilius) DVPLICARIVS / ALA PRIMA TRACVM PAGO / SARDI(ca) ANNO(rum) XL ANNOR(um) XV / HEREDES EXS TESTAM(ento) [F(aciendum)] C(uraverunt) / H(ic) S(itus) E(st)

Longinus Sdapeze, son of Matycus, *duplicarius* from the first *ala* of Thracians, from the district of Sardica, aged 40, of 15 years' service, lies buried here. His heirs under his will had set this up. (Campbell 1994, p. 54/*RIB* 201)

Reconstruction of an oval *clipeus* (Corinium Museum, Cirencester), the characteristic flat shield carried by auxiliary infantrymen and cavalrymen alike. An oval *clipeus* was only slightly lighter than a cylindrical *scutum* – its greater height compensating for the latter's greater width. (© Nic Fields)

Longius Sdapeze, a Thracian, came from Sardica, that is, Sofia, the capital of modern Bulgaria. As he was a non-citizen (he would have gained this on his honourable discharge, if he had not died, after 25 years' service in the *auxilia*), we notice he lacks the *tria nomina* (i.e. *praenomen*, *nomen* and *cognomen*) common to Roman citizens. An examination of the extant epitaphs reveals that many soldiers did not see the end of their full-term of enlistment; not only was the mortality rate higher in antiquity, but the life of a soldier had ever a tinge of the hazardous.

Tacitus talks of a Cohors Sugambrorum under Tiberius, as 'savage as the enemy in its chanting and clashing of arms' (*Ann.* 4.47.4), although fighting far from its Germanic homeland in Thrace. Further information concerning these tribal levies comes from Tacitus' account of the ruinous civil war. In AD 69, when Vitellius marched into Rome as the next short-lived emperor, his army also included 34 *cohortes* 'grouped according to nationality and type of equipment' (*Hist.* 2.89.2).

Take the members of Cohors II Tungrorum, for instance, who had been originally raised from among the Tungri, who inhabited the north-western fringes of the Arduenna Silva (Ardennes Forest) in Gallia

Belgica. Under the Iulio-Claudian emperors, it was quite common for such units to be stationed in or near the province where they were first raised. However, the anarchic events of AD 69, when a large proportion of the *auxilia* serving on the Rhine frontier mutinied, led to a change in this policy. Thereafter, though the Roman high command would not abandon local recruiting, it would stop the practice of keeping units with so continuous an ethnic identity close to their homelands, instead posting them to provinces far away from home.

Auxiliary cohorts were 480 strong (*quingenaria* – 'five-hundred strong'); *milliaria* ('one-thousand strong') units would not appear until around AD 70. Known as *cohortes peditata*, these infantry units had six centuries with 80 soldiers to each, and, as in the legions, a centurion and an *optio* commanded a century, which was likewise divided into ten *contubernia*.

Tacitus talks of Augustus forming Ala Batavorum, a cavalry unit commanded by a Batavian chieftain, Chariovalda, which fought for Rome during the trans-Rhenish campaigns of Germanicus from AD 14 to AD 16 (*Ann.* 2.8, 2.11). The *auxilia* cavalry units were known as *alae* ('wings'), which originally denoted the allies (*socii*) posted on the flanks of the consular armies of the middle Republic. In our period of study, they were *quingenaria* (512 in total), and are thought to have consisted of 16 *turmae* (Hyginus 16; cf. *CIL* iii.6581), each with 30 troopers (Fink 1971, p. 80; cf. Arr. *Takt.* 18.3), commanded by a *decurio equitum* and his second-in-command, the *duplicarius*. Drawn from peoples nurtured in the saddle – Gauls, Germans, Iberians and Thracians were preferred – the horsemen of the *alae* provided a fighting arm in which the Romans were not so adept.

Additionally, there were mixed foot/horse units, the *cohortes equitatae*. Their internal organization is less clear, but usually assumed, following Hyginus (26–27), to have six centuries of 80 men and four *turmae* of 30 troopers, that is to say, *cohors equitata quingenaria* (608 in total). An inscription, dated to the reign of Tiberius, mentions a *praefectus cohortis Ubiorum peditum et equitum* (prefect of a cohort of Ubii, foot and horse – *ILS* 2690), which is probably the earliest example of this type of mixed unit. Parenthetically, it is worth noting that this Tiberian auxiliary unit was recruited from the Ubii, originally a trans-Rhenish Germanic tribe distinguished for its loyalty to Rome (Tac. *Ger.* 28.4); the Ubii, as allies of Rome, were given permission in 38 BC or 16 BC to settle around what was to become Colonia Agrippinensis–Cologne on the west bank of the Rhine.

The remains of three rectangular repoussé plaques (Musée d'archéologie nationale, Saint-Germain-en-Laye), each decorated with a bust (Tiberius?) and two cornucopia, from the sépulture de Chassenard, département du l'Allier, dated to the last years of Tiberius (narrow rectangular plaques are typical of Augustan and Tiberian periods). These would have adorned a *cingulum militaris* (belt) of the interred Gaulish *decurio* (officer). Associated with the plaques is a belt buckle decorated with embossed motifs too. (© Esther Carré)

(Left) Legionary *pugio* (Archäologisches Museum, Gunzenhausen). Dagger blades were relatively thin, and the ridges and grooves increased their strength. (Right) Reconstruction of a legionary *pugio* made by a member of Legio XXI Rapax re-enactment group, on display at Sechseläuten 2011, Lindenhof, 11 April 2011. A *pugio* was regarded as a personal weapon and a tool, and its hilt and scabbard decoration subject to an individual's taste (and purse). It seems even ordinary rankers were quite prepared to invest considerable sums on decorated daggers and scabbards. (Left, Wolfgang Sauber/Wikimedia Commons/CC-BY-SA-3.0; right, Roland zh/Wikimedia Commons/CC-BY-SA-3.0)

In Gaul, Caesar had employed Germanic horse warriors who could fight in conjunction with foot warriors, operating in pairs (Caes. *B Gall.* 7.65.5, 8.36.4; cf. Tac. *Ger.* 6.2). During the civil war, they served him again. In one battle, Caesar ordered his lightly armed Germani, both foot and horse (*Germanos levis armaturae equitumque*), to cross a river, while in another, *equites Germani* reportedly swam across a river at points where the banks were lower (Caes. *B civ.* 1.83.5, *B Alex.* 29.2). It is worth taking a moment to note that these Germani serving Caesar were adept at crossing rivers, a speciality of the Batavian *auxilia* in the early principate (more of which later).

Organized, disciplined and well trained, the pride of the Roman cavalry were obviously the horsemen of the *alae*, but more numerous were the horsemen of the *cohortes equitatae*. Having served for some time as infantrymen before being upgraded and trained as cavalrymen, these troopers were not as highly paid, or as well mounted as their brothers of the *alae*, but they performed many of the day-to-day patrolling, policing and escort duties.

In addition, as in earlier times, there were specialists fulfilling roles in which Roman citizens, better utilized as legionaries, were traditionally unskilled. Among the Romans, like the Greeks before them, the bow seems never to have been held in much favour, though after the time of Marius, it was introduced by Cretan mercenaries serving Rome. Cassius Dio (62.12.4) mentions archers serving with Suetonius Paulinus in Britannia during the Boudican rebellion, but he adds no details. However, the best known of these specialists were archers from Syria. It is possible they were equipped as regular auxiliaries, rather than in the exotic eastern appearance indicated on Trajan's Column (First Dacian War, Scene 70/LXX; Second Dacian War, scenes 108/CVIII, 115/CXV), which clearly depicts them with high cheekbones and aquiline noses, wearing voluminous flowing skirts that swing round their ankles. Certainly 1st-century AD funerary *stelae* show archers in the customary off-duty uniform of woollen tunic with *gladius* and *pugio* belts (*cinguli*), crossed 'cowboy' fashion. Whether or not these experts with the composite recurve bow were part of the Claudian invasion force, we do not know.

THE BRITONS

It should be stressed from the beginning that there probably never was a typical Iron Age British warrior. Insular Iron Age studies increasingly point to substantial differences in the material culture, and, therefore, we assume in the everyday life of the people inhabiting Iron Age Britain. Strabo, writing in the Augustan age, has this to say regarding the Britons:

> The men of Britannia are taller than the Gauls and not so yellowed-haired. Their bodies are more loosely built. This will give you an idea of their size: I myself in Rome saw youths standing half a foot taller than the tallest in the city, although they were bandy-legged and ungainly in build. (Strab. 4.5.2)

Who the Celts actually were, and indeed if they existed as a recognizable ethnic entity, is a lively topic of debate, at least among some archaeologists. With regards to Britannia, the whole question is neatly dismissed by Tacitus: 'Be this as it may, what race of mortal birth inhabited Britannia originally, whether native to the soil or later comers, is a question which, as one would expect among barbarous people, has never received attention' (*Agr.* 11.1).

Foul hordes

For our purposes, it is sufficient to say that the peoples the Greeks and the Romans called the Keltoi/Celtae had a fearsome reputation for aggressiveness, even among the militaristic Romans, and there can be no doubt that warfare played a central role in Iron Age Celtic society – a society that was tribal, hierarchical and familiar. For the nobles and their warrior retainers, raiding neighbouring tribes offered the opportunity of wealth, prestige and reputation to further political aspirations at home. Retinues could only be maintained by actual fighting, and they seem to have been at least semi-permanent and, added to their clients, formed a strong nucleus for the tribal army. Polybios, writing of the Celts much earlier, comments that the nobility 'treated comradeship as of great importance, those among them being the most feared and most powerful who were thought to have the largest number of attendants and associates' (2.17.12). These elite warriors were, however, far outnumbered by the mass of common warriors, composed of all free tribesmen able to equip themselves to the best of their ability, and here we have to remember that the majority of the followers of Caratacus and Togodumnus, even though bound to a local chieftain by the dues of patron–client relationships, were farmers who planted crops and raised cattle. There would have been a few raw adolescents and greying men feeling their years too.

As these tribesmen appear to have gone to war in bands based on clan, familiar and settlement groupings (which made a man's people the witness of his battlefield behaviour), it is likely too that the boldest (or more foolhardy) and best equipped naturally gravitated to the front rank of a war band (Rawlings 1996, p. 90; Goldsworthy 1998, p. 59). Individual warriors were motivated not so much by the ends of the battle as the means. Equipment in general was fairly scanty, the combination of shield, long slashing sword and short thrusting spear(s) forming the war gear of most common warriors. Body armour seems to have been very rare, the wearing of mail shirts being restricted to the warrior elite. The common warrior almost certainly went into battle dressed only in a pair of loose woollen trousers (*bracae*).

Celtic charge

The appearance of the individual, his size, expressions and demoniacal war cries, added to the din of clashing weapons and the harsh braying of the carnyx (animal-headed war horn), were clearly intended to intimidate the enemy before actually reaching them. Diodorus Siculus says: 'their trumpets are of a peculiar kind, they blow into them and produce a harsh sound that suits

A Celtic horned helmet, British Museum, London (inv. P&E 1988 10-4.1), La Tène D (150–1 BC). This item was dredged from the bed of the Thames at Waterloo Bridge, London in the early 1860s. Made from sheet bronze, the helmet is held together with many carefully placed bronze rivets. It remains the only helmet to be found in southern Britain, and though there are examples surmounted with fantastic crests, it is the only Iron Age helmet with horns to be found anywhere in Europe. Horns are often the symbol of the gods. (WordRidden/ Wikimedia Commons/ CC-BY-SA-2.0)

Meyrick Helmet (British Museum, London, inv. 1872, 1213.2) – a bronze peaked helmet in the 'jockey-cap' style, 1st century AD. The conical cap is largely adorned with repoussé (raised decoration hammered through the reverse side) while the peaked neck guard was once richly adorned with enamel and glass. Insular Iron Age art reached a magnificent peak, especially in metalwork, all swirling motifs and fine enamelling. There is a hole at the top of the helmet for the attachment of a plumed topknot. The helmet was made from a single sheet of copper alloy, possibly spun finished. (Geni/Wikimedia Commons/ CC-BY-SA-4.0)

the tumult of war' (5.30.3). Such brouhaha was sufficiently startling and cacophonous to set the enemy on an edge, as the Romans were when they faced a coalition of Cisalpine Gauls at Telamon (Polyb. 2.29.5–9); and if he was persuaded it was better to run scared than to get run over before an actual mêlée began, then a Celtic charge, oftentimes launched without warning, would drive all before it. However, the Romans tended to out-endure the less well-protected and disciplined Celts if they weathered the initial ferocity of their rush.

Tactics – if tactics we may call them – were therefore unsophisticated, and relied on a wild, headlong rush by a yelling mass of warriors in a rough phalangial block headed by their war leaders, followed up by deadly close-up work with short ashen spear and long slashing sword. As was common in tribal armies, the common warriors, unmilitary but exceedingly warlike, were poorly disciplined and lacked training above the level of the individual. And so after a violent and savage onslaught launched amid a colossal din, the individual warrior battered his way into the enemy's ranks, punching with his shield, and stabbing with his spear or slashing with his sword. The muscular agility of Celtic warriors was a thing to behold, and those on the opposing side could only stand like pebbles on a beach, waiting for the smothering surge.

One certain thing about the resistance army of Caratacus and Togodumnus: It was a rambunctious host, containing as its flower some of the best manpower available – raw-boned, sinewy men used to handling weapons and to the outdoor life, men who could get along very well on poor rations and skimpy equipment, bands of free tribesmen, who, as they always seem to be in history, were fit, agile and extremely belligerent men with a positive taste for fighting. Like all tribal warriors, they were shrewd, quick-witted, wary, cunning and ready for all emergencies, and while there was no attempt at discipline, their courage was tempestuous, excitable and self-conscious. Yet we should always remember that only an adolescent without wife or wains would leap into battle careless of his fate.

Chasing chariots

So much for the generalities concerning Celtic armies. In the early encounters of Celt and Roman, even though the bulk of a Celtic tribal host fought on foot, it was the chariot that roused the curiosity of the Romans. 'In warfare they use chariots', explains Strabo (4.5.2). Pulled by two yoked horses and driven by skilled charioteers, it appears that the main use of the Celtic war chariot was for causing panic. The charioteers, who normally sat rather than stood, would drive their light-framed vehicles against the enemy lines in a rush, sparring and skirmishing, the accompanying warriors scattering and throwing spears as they did so; and this, coupled with the mere speed and noise of the dashing chariots, would be enough to unsettle the opposition.

Tacitus, during the retelling of the Battle of Mons Graupius (precise location unknown), says that prior to the general engagement, 'the flat space between the two armies was taken up by the noisy manoeuvring of the charioteers' (*Agr.* 35.3). As the chariot warriors were standing upright, with the extra advantage of height and close proximity to the enemy, hitting their targets was made that much easier. Once this initial phase had been accomplished, the warriors could choose to step off their chariots to fight afoot, as in the manner of the heroes of the *Iliad*, while the charioteers kept the chariots at the ready to execute, if necessary, a speedy retreat, as admirably described by Caesar (*B Gall.* 4.33.2, see below). Enigmatically, Tacitus says of the two-man chariot crew that 'the charioteer has the place of honour, the combatants are mere retainers' (*Agr.* 12.1). It is possible that the Caledonii employed tactics different from those that Caesar had encountered in the south of the mainland island some 130 years before.

It was Diodorus Siculus who noted that the tribes of Britannia 'used chariots as tradition tells us the old Greek heroes did in the Trojan War' (5.21.5). Admittedly, Diodorus was on the lookout for Homeric parallels in Celtic society, and his account is somewhat anachronistic and admitted to be based upon hearsay. Despite this, however, Diodorus' statement can be expanded and elucidated upon by referring to the source from which it probably came, Caesar's *commentarii*. Caesar had a keen eye for the extraordinary, and his eyewitness battlefield report of Britannic charioteers in action presents a marvellous picture of their skill and agility. What Caesar says deserves to be quoted in full:

Terracotta statuette (Ashmolean Museum, Oxford) of a warrior sporting a distinctively Celtic hairstyle, drooping moustache, trousers and tunic, along with a sheathed long slashing sword suspended on his right hip, and a shield with an axial spine and central strip boss. According to the Augustan geographer Strabo, the Celts had 'a thing peculiar to them, that they endeavour not to grow fat or pot-bellied, and any young man who exceeds the standard measure of the girdle is punished' (4.4.6). Presumably, this obese warrior was either too fond of his food to care or beyond the age of censure. (Carole Raddato/Wikimedia Commons/CC-BY-SA-2.0)

> In chariot fighting, the Britons begin by riding all over the field hurling javelins, and generally the terror inspired by the horses and the noise of the wheels are sufficient to throw their opponents' ranks into disorder. Then, after making their way between the cavalry squadrons, they jump down from their chariots and engage on foot. (2) In the meantime their charioteers retire a short distance from the battle and place the chariots in such a position that their warriors, if hard pressed by numbers, have an easy means of retreat to their own lines. (3) Thus they combine the mobility of cavalry with the staying power of infantry; and by daily training and practice they attain such proficiency that even on a steep incline, they are able to control the horses at a full gallop, and to check and turn them in a moment. They can run along the chariot pole, stand on the yoke and get back into the chariot as quick as lightning. (Caes. *B Gall.* 4.33.1–3)

There is, of course, the problem as to whether the author meant their own cavalry squadrons or those of the enemy, though *equitum turmes* in all likelihood refers to the Roman cavalry. For example, Livy (10.28–30), although he provides no details, tells us that at Sentinum (295 BC) the Senonian Gauls deployed a thousand chariots, and these counter-attacked and routed the Roman cavalry, which was pursuing the broken Gaulish cavalry of the right flank. The chariots then pursued in turn, following the routed Roman

cavalry into the ranks of the Roman infantry. Seeing the legionaries thus disordered, the Gaulish war bands charged and pushed the Romans back. Likewise, Tacitus tells us that at the zenith of the fighting at Mons Graupius (AD 83), the Roman cavalry *turmae* 'had routed the war chariots' (*Agr.* 36.2). Besides, if Caesar's chariot warriors are infiltrating their own cavalry, whom are they supposed to be fighting?

Iron Age Cantiaci coin from Kent (Find ID: 312418). The obverse (left) bears a bust with the legend AMMI. The reverse (right) bears a facing chariot with two horses and a charioteer, with the letters E and C (above) and S (below); perhaps SEG[O]? Sego is thought to mean 'power'. In continental Europe, the last recorded use of chariots in war was in 225 BC at Telamon, on the coast of northern Etruria. (The Portable Antiquities Scheme/The Trustees of the British Museum/ Wikimedia Commons/CC-BY-SA-2.0)

Britannic chariots were certainly not designed to crash through those opposing them, and one of their main weaknesses was the vulnerability of the horses that drew them, such large targets being an easy prey to those armed with missile or throwing weapons, as shall be witnessed when we discuss the Battle of the Medway (Dio 60.20.3). On the contrary, one of their preferred ploys was probably the feigned retreat, to draw off small parties of the enemy, who could then be tackled by the chariot warriors leaping down to fight hand to hand. The paired horses, swift-turning and sure-footed, were obviously specially bred and trained to pull war chariots, for which purpose a low wither height was preferable. They were probably similar to the Exmoor pony, the oldest of the native British horse.

In Caesar's vivid description, only the stunt of running out along the chariot pole to stand on the yoke is non-Homeric. Still, the chariot he witnessed in Britannia was open at its front face, thereby allowing the chariot warrior to perform such an acrobatic feat. Undoubtedly, to do so invited danger: Arviragus (or Arvirargus), an otherwise unknown Britannic king

Wetwang chariot reconstruction by the Somerset wheelwright Robert Hurford. He cleverly devised a suspension system that employed two sets of flexible ash-wood arches, from which hung thongs of braided rawhide. This arrangement suspended a strapwork riding platform, which in turn was attached to the chassis below it by flexible leather straps. The traction power was provided by two yoked horses, a Welsh Pony (Nugget) and a Dartmoor cross (Fudge), both with a wither height of more or less 112cm, or 11 hands. Generally speaking, with small horse breeds, you harness to a chariot; as soon as you can breed bigger horses, you ride them. The Celtic chariot was small and light, combining speed and manoeuvrability. (Courtesy of Mike Loades)

(he is mentioned by Geoffrey of Monmouth, and makes an appearance in Shakespeare's *Cymbeline*), is said to have been hurled from a chariot pole (Juv. *Sat.* 4.126–27). The Homeric chariot, as far as we can tell, had a cab enclosed on three sides, made up of a heat-bent wooden frame, which probably stood at waist height or thereabouts. If this was the case, then running out along the chariot pole was not an option for Diodorus' Greek heroes when they fought their epic battles.

Evidence for the La Tène chariot is derived from pictorial representations, such as an Etruscan funerary stele from Padua, carved in or around the 3rd century BC; and late Republican Roman denarii, which help to provide information concerning the wooden and leather parts that no longer survive; and excavation work, such as the vehicle burials of Yorkshire, which more often than not renders the actual metal components. Let us take one of these vehicle burials as emblematic, namely the two-wheeled chariot-like construction (chariot, cart or carriage?) unearthed at the Iron Age cemetery at Wetwang Slack, East Riding of Yorkshire, in the summer of 1984.

The large spoked wheels had been removed from the vehicle and laid flat on the floor of the grave pit. The skeleton of a warrior rested on the wheels, and was accompanied by an iron slashing sword in a bronze and iron scabbard, a clutch of no fewer than seven spearheads, which were scattered across the body, and fragments of the iron spine of a shield. Laid on one of the wheels were two iron horse bits; on the other, a line of five bronze and iron terrets (rein-guiding rings) marked the position of the yoke of the vehicle. As you would expect, the wooden and leather parts of the vehicle had all rotted away, but the wooden components, such as the chariot pole, were located by filling the voids left behind with plaster or by recording the darker stains left in the soil of the excavation by wood tannins, such as the spokes of the two wheels. The two iron tyres survived in good condition.

The case of the Britannic chariot offers an interesting example. The kind of vehicles Caesar describes so well must have had special qualities such as lightness for speed and quick turning, yet toughness to stand up to the rough going and heavy usage. The open back allowed the chariot to be rapidly boarded or dismounted on the field of battle. Thus, the chariot could be boarded from behind, but was also open at the front so the charioteer could be seated. As Caesar mentions, the chariot warrior could run along the chariot pole to slash at enemies before the chariot.

Clearly, with this sort of acrobatics, good suspension was all-important, for Britain is not noted for its table-flat terrain. As Flavius Arrianus makes clear in a passage comparing the armoured scythe-bearing chariots of the Persians and those used by the Britons:

> The latter generally use pairs of small scruffy horses. Their two-horse chariots are suitable for driving in all kinds of locales and their ponies [τὰ ἱππάρια] are suitable for doing harsh labour. (Arr. *Takt.* 19.3)

Some form of strap-work floor structure therefore would have made practical sense. On the aforementioned Paduan stele and late republican Roman denarii, we see La Tène chariots with open-work double-arched sides, each depicted with a Y configuration inside. It has been suggested that this Y was actually

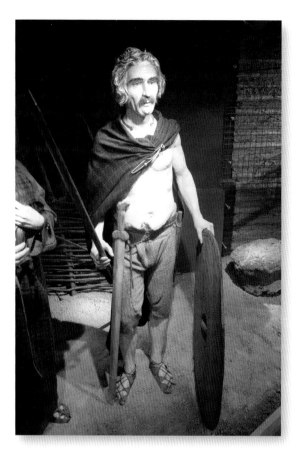

Life-size manikin of a Celtic warrior (Muzeum Archeologiczne, Kraków). Free men of fewer means, the warrior farmers who formed the military backbone of Celtic war bands, were without armour. They were almost certainly armed with a plank shield for protection, either oval or hexagonal and ranging in height from 1.1m to 1.4m, an ashen spear for thrusting and a long iron sword for slashing. These men usually went into battle dressed only in a pair of loose trousers, or *bracae*. These common warriors were not all young, muscle-bound heroes. (Šilar/Wikimedia Commons/CC-BY-SA-3.0)

a thong of braided rawhide, which suspended an independent riding platform inside the cab frame and free of the wheels and the axle. These thongs were probably hung from two sets of flexible ash arches. Field trials, using a full-scale replica of the Wetwang vehicle unearthed in the spring of 2001, proved the independent or 'floating' suspension system quite literally suspends. More importantly, it worked. It was this vehicle that was used as the basis for an experimental reconstruction in the BBC series *Meet the Ancestors*, and according to Mike Loades, 'it was possible to either sit or stand at walk, trot, canter and gallop over rough, bumpy terrain. It was even possible to throw javelins from the moving vehicle and hit targets of cardboard Romans' (2005). The trials proved that the floating suspension system gave the chariot crew a much smoother ride, even when moving at speed over rugged terrain.

To judge from his silence, chariots were no longer in fashion when Caesar was busy conquering Gaul, and he was somewhat surprised to find them still in use by the tribes of south-eastern Britannia, a surprise that engendered the aforementioned commentary. As their prowess and agility as horsemen increased, so the Gauls gradually gave up the war chariot. In Britannia, on the other hand, they were still used in numbers. In one engagement, Caesar (*B Gall.* 5.19.1) claims his adversary Cassivellaunus commanded no fewer than 4,000 chariots (perhaps something of an exaggeration), which were used to devastating effect against the Romans. Chariots were to make their appearance again during the Boudican rebellion of AD 60–61, and in the final battle of Mons Graupius, in which Agricola shattered the resistance of the Caledonii in the far north of Britannia in AD 83. The discovery in 2001 of a chariot burial at Newbridge, Midlothian, confirms the existence of chariots in Iron Age Scotland. Writing of the Severan campaign of AD 208–10, Cassius Dio records that the Caledonii and Maeatae 'go into battle in chariots, and have small, swift horses' (76.12.3). This is the last recorded historical reference to the use of chariots in warfare in Britannia. According to early Irish epic literature, chariots survived for several centuries on the battlefields of Ireland.

If we return to Diodorus Siculus, we are offered by him a description of the possible tactical role of the La Tène chariot, as was earlier used by the tribes of Gaul:

> In their travels and when they go into battle, the Gauls use chariots drawn by two horses, which carry the charioteer and the warrior; and when they encounter cavalry in the fighting, they first hurl their javelins at the enemy, and then step down from their chariots and join battle with their swords …
> (2) They bring with them as retainers freemen enrolled from among the poor, whom they used as charioteers and shield bearers in battle. (3) And when the

armies are drawn up against each other, it is their custom to come forward from the line of battle and challenge the noblest of their adversaries to single combat, brandishing their weapons before them and striking terror into the enemy. (Diod. Sic. 5.29.1–3)

All in all, the tactical role of the La Tène chariot can be divided into three basic tactical functions. First, prior to battle being joined, the chariot warriors hurl their throwing spears. Second, having performed this initial task, the chariot warriors dismount to fight on foot (being nobles, they could step into no-man's-land and issue challenges to enemy champions for individual demonstrations of tour de force). Third, in the meantime, the charioteers retire a safe distance in case they are needed for a swift pursuit or hurried retreat. Additionally, though of course La Tène chariots were not designed for charging headlong into a well-formed enemy formation, there is no tactical reason why they would not be driven into shaken formations, which are likely to flinch and fail, or have the ability to run down fleeing fugitives.

Tall, terrifying and tattooed

'Do not cut your bodies for the dead or put tattoo marks on yourselves. I am the LORD.' So runs one of the prohibitions handed down to Moses and eventually listed in the Book of Leviticus (19:28 NIV). The key principle here is God does not want His people to be idolatrous.

A number of modern scholars, with an Iudaeo-Christian propensity to directly associate the practice with punishment, subjection, low social status and feeble-mindedness, have been rather reluctant to credit the accounts of tattooing among the Britons, which are found among the Graeco-Roman sources. In a reaction akin to being poked in the eye with a sharp stick, they prefer to believe that the authors simply made it up and/or got it wrong. This is patently untrue.

The public at large, on the other hand, is less sceptical of and less put off by the image of the ancient Britons wearing tattoos, because of changes in British culture. In fact, with tattoos currently fashionable, many people now desire the ancient Britons to have been thickset, powerfully built men, handsomely moustached, and painted or tattooed. Yet no Graeco-Roman writer makes the claim that the Celts, generally speaking, were painted or tattooed; on the other hand, there is evidence in Graeco-Roman sources that tattooing was customary among at least some Britannic tribes.

Even though the Greeks and Romans had heard of the 'barbarian' Celts, they first

(Above) Mouth of an Iron Age Celtic war trumpet known as the carnyx (National of Museums Scotland, Edinburgh), found in a peat bog near Deskford, Banffshire (1816), and dated to the mid-1st century AD. Wrought in sheet bronze, it is in the manner of a stylized boar's head. The open mouth would have held a wooden tongue, which rattled when it vibrated and was designed to terrify the enemy by its cacophonic noise. (Below) An American re-enactor dressed as a Briton equipped with a carnyx and replica Battersea helmet. (Above, © Esther Carré; below, Kabuto 7/Wikimedia Commons/CC-BY-SA-4.0)

The well-known Celtic shield (British Museum, London, inv. P&E 1857 7-13.1) dredged from the bed of the Thames at Battersea Bridge (1857), dated to La Tène B (380–250 BC). Being both too short (<0.9m long) and too flimsy to offer reasonable protection, this shield (facing), with its brazen polish and scarlet glass, had no place on the battlefield, and was probably meant for flamboyant display as opposed to practical combat use. Consisting of restless, swelling patterns and gaudy enamelling, the spectacular decoration is typically in the insular La Tène style. It had undoubtedly served as a water offering to some chthonic deity. (QuartierLatin1968/Wikimedia Commons/CC-BY-SA-3.0)

encountered them as warriors, and it was on the red field of battle that their enormous size and outlandish appearance first struck them, usually with terror. The Celtic chieftains who advanced to challenge their opposing Roman leader to single combat as a prelude to the general mêlée were muscle-bound, hirsute warriors who swung big iron swords. The Celts were generally striking in demeanour because of their great height (by Mediterranean standards, they stood a head taller), yellowish or reddish hair, shaggy appearance and pale complexions. Descriptions of hair that was slaked with lime and combed back to make it stick up like a horse's mane specifically refer to the Gauls (Diod. Sic. 5.28.2), but it is reasonable to suggest that the Britons may have lime-tipped their hair in this fashion too. It should be noted the use of lime had a secondary effect, that is to say, it tended to bleach the hair. The Celts themselves took great pride in their appearance, to impress each other and to alarm their foes on the field of battle; it was a source of pleasure for them.

Herodian, recounting the campaigns of Septimius Severus against the Caledonii (AD 208–10), says that they went about unclothed and barefooted, and there are many earlier references to the Celtic habit of rushing naked into battle (Polyb. 2.28.8, 30.1, 3.114.4; Diod. Sic. 5.29.2, 30.3; Livy 38.21.9, 26.7), though these same sources also depict the Celts naked only from the waist up (Polyb. 2.28.7; Livy 22.46.6). Interestingly enough, Herodian concludes by saying that the Caledonii did not wish to cover up the artwork on their bodies, having tattooed (he uses a form of the Greek verb στίζειν, literally 'to prick') them with 'various designs and pictures of all kinds of animals' (3.14.7). Animals are the most frequent subject matter of tattooing in many cultures, and are traditionally associated with magic, totems and the desire of the tattooed person to become identified with the spirit of the animal. All of the known Pazyryk tattoos (see below) are images of animals.

To Herodian's comments may be added a poem from Claudian (22.248; cf. 26.417), which, though written relatively late, also mentions tattooing (*ferro picta*, literally 'iron-marked'), as does Jordanes (*fl.* AD 550), who says the Caledonii had *ferro pingunt corpora*, 'iron-painted bodies' (*Get.* 2.14). Presumably, the use of these two phrases refers to the use of a sharp iron point to pierce the skin, allowing the dye on its tip to be introduced under the skin through the resulting puncture.

Tattooing may well have identified the tribe and the status of the wearer. 'Scars that speak', in modern parlance – or as a Maori once put it to an outsider, 'You may be robbed of your prized possessions but of your moko (facial tattoo) you cannot be deprived' (quoted in Caplan 2000, p. 251). It has been argued (Diack 1944, p. 28) that Tacitus' enigmatic reference to the Caledonii, 'famous warriors wearing their several decorations' (*Agr.* 29.2), was a reference to their social status or tribal identity displayed in the form of tattoos. This was certainly the academic opinion of Isidorus Hispalensis (d. AD 636) when he was referring to the Picts of his day:

> The race of the Picts (Picti) has a name derived from the appearance of their bodies. These are played upon by a needle working with small pricks (*quod minutis opifex acus punctis*) and by the squeezed-out sap of a native plant, so that they bear the resultant marks according to the personal rank of the individual, their painted limbs being tattooed to show their high birth. (Isid. *Etym.* 19.23.7)

Justifiably, it must be said, the debate concerning Pictish tattooing is closely linked to that surrounding the name of the Picts. As Claudian himself pointed out, *noc falso nomine Pictos*, 'the well-named Picts' (6.54).

But what can we say about the more southerly Britannic tribes? In almost all his campaigns in Gaul, Caesar (*B Gall.* 4.20.1) had noticed Britons fighting in Gaulish armies. It is unclear how Caesar managed to distinguish Britannic warriors from Gaulish ones, although we can reasonably guess that the Britannic habit of tattooing the body may have led to their positive identification amongst the enemy ranks. Yet, unlike the discovery by Soviet and Russian archaeologists of the Pazyryk bodies (including one female) with extensive tattoo work, no Briton's skin has ever been found emblazoned with tattoos. On the other hand, we do have Caesar's remarks about the painted bodies of the Britons he faced during his second visit to Britannia.

Clearly fascinated, Caesar says: 'all the Brittanni dye their bodies with *vitrum*, which produces a bluish colour and gives them a wild appearance in battle' (*B Gall.* 5.14.4). The verb Caesar uses for the process is *inficere*, to stain or dye as oppose to puncturing (viz. permanent and penetrative), and his account gains credence from the recent discovery of clay-based copper pigment in the skin of Lindow III, a second male (headless) body found in February 1987 and dated to AD 30–225. Pomponius Mela (*fl.* AD 43) also describes painted Britons, and, like Caesar, calls the pigment *vitrum*, 'glass, crystal' (*De situ orbis* 3.6.51). This is not woad (Lat. *Isatis tinctoria*, OE *wād*), a plant belonging to the mustard family (Brassicaceae) that yields the blue dye indigo and called *glastum* by Pliny (*HN* 22.2.2), but a copper-based pigment, such as malachite or azurite, which produces a blue-green pigment for body marking. Woad was certainly known and used by the Britons, but probably for its antiseptic properties; Old English textual citations suggest smearing *wād* on burns, not using it as a dye.

Caesar may have provided the inspiration for Augustan poetic allusions to blue-painted Britons, one by Propertius and the other by Ovid. Whereas Propertius merely refers to *infectos … Britannos*, 'the painted Briton' (2.18C.1; cf. Mar. *Epigr.* 11.53.1, 14.99, and Sil. *Pun.* 17.416), Ovid speaks of *vitreos Britannos*, 'glassy Britons' (*Am.* 2.16.39).

Another alternative, of course, is the very ancient art of tattooing. The first possible tattoos in history date back to over 5,300 years ago, to the several soot tattoos on Ötzi the

Celtic swords (British Museum, London), dated to La Tène D (150–1 BC). These were blunt-ended long iron swords, wide, flat, tapering and double-edged, designed for fighting in open order, where they could be swung effectively to slash into or fell an adversary's body. Improvements in iron technology and changes in fighting style resulted in slashing swords of often-enormous length in the 2nd and 1st centuries BC. Perhaps surprisingly, they were worn on the right, suspended from a waist belt of metal chain, which passed through a loop on the back of the iron scabbard. It is in fact fairly easy to draw even a long blade from this position. (Völkerwanderer/Wikimedia Commons/CC0-1.0)

Iceman, a glacial mummy from the Copper Age found in the Ötztal Alps straddling Austria and Italy in October 1991. Normally, the skin is punctured, scored or cut with a very sharp or pointed instrument. A tool such as a bone awl with its needle-sharp point would have been ideal for the task. A colour paste was then rubbed into the skin. The pigment most frequently used was powdered charcoal (in Ötzi's case it was manufactured out of soot), stirred up with saliva or tepid freshwater, which produces the familiar blue tint. Tattooing appears to be the crux of observation made by Caius Iulius Solinus, an avid collector of curious facts writing in the early 3rd century AD – he was a contemporary of Herodian – when he said:

> For the most part, Britannia is held by barbarians. Even from childhood, they are marked by local artists with various figures and images of animals. When a man's body has been *inscribed* [author's emphasis], the marks of the pigment increase with growth. The wild nations in this place consider nothing to be greater proof of patience than that through the unforgetful scars, their bodies may drink in the most dye [*fucus*]. (Solinus *Polyhistorae* 22.12)

The fact remains, of course, in the academic circle there are contrary schools of thought with strongly differing opinions, and contradictory research, on whether or not facial and corporeal dying, painting and tattooing was culturally practised by the insular Iron Age Celts and/or the early medieval Picts, the latter a people still best known for their carved stone monuments.

One final point, one in fact based on onomastics: It is interesting to note that the original inhabitants of the land the Romans called Britannia (Gk. Pretanníа) knew it as Albion (Plin. *HN* 4.16.102) and themselves as Pretani or Priteni, which possibly meant 'people of the designs' (MacQuarrie 1999). The name survived as Picti, Picts (cf. the Welsh for Britain – Prydain). It was long believed that the name Picti originated as a derisory nickname first coined by the Romans from the late 3rd century AD onwards to describe the tattooed/painted inhabitants of northern Britannia beyond what had been the Antonine Wall (e.g. *Pan. Lat.* 8.11.4; Amm. Marc. 20.1.1, 26.4.5, 27.8.5). It is now thought the name is of indigenous origin instead, with the Picti being a super tribe or a loose confederation of people.

OPPOSING PLANS

The Claudian invasion of AD 43 was politically motivated to meet the aspirations of an emperor recently dragged from his academic obscurity to fulfil the need for a dynast of the Iulio-Claudian family. His name, Tiberius Claudius Nero Germanicus, may have been illustriously lengthy, but his position as emperor was initially insecure, and his most obvious failing was his lack of military prestige, a view promoted by Suetonius (*Claud.* 17.1). As a keen antiquarian – he was physically rather than mentally disabled – Claudius astutely foresaw the propaganda value of an invasion and annexation of Britannia, which would enable him to emulate one of the most renowned exploits of that masterly impresario, Caesar, and at the same time win for himself military glory.

True, it is also arguable that there was a genuine political justification for the campaign: local factional squabbles threatened to disrupt lucrative trade, providing an acceptable excuse for military intervention. After all, the Romans used superior military might and physical control of territory to project their imperial interests in the Mediterranean heartlands, while *divide et impera* ('divide and rule') was the operative coin of the Roman Empire. Though the divide-to-conquer policy was essential to imperial success, we must not lose sight of the elaborate preparations for the involvement in the final stages of the campaign of Claudius himself, along with his elephants, which surely hint strongly at the underlying propaganda pull of the whole

(Left) Fused remains of *lorica hamata* (Musée d'archéologie nationale, Saint-Germain-en-Laye, inv. 50188), recovered from the sépulture de Chassenard, département du l'Allier, dated to the last years of Tiberius. Discovered in 1874, the burial probably belonged to a Gaulish *decurio* – the funerary offerings included a face helmet – who commanded one of the *turmae* in an auxiliary cavalry unit. (Right) Modern reconstruction of *lorica hamata*. Although mail had two very considerable drawbacks – it was extremely laborious to make, and while it afforded complete freedom of movement to the wearer, it was very heavy (this example weighs 12kg) – such armour was popular. A mail shirt was flexible and essentially shapeless, fitting more closely to the wearer's body than other types of armour. In this respect it was comfortable, whilst the wearing of a belt helped to spread its considerable weight, which would otherwise be carried entirely by the shoulders. Mail offered reasonable protection, but could be penetrated by a strong thrust or an arrow fired at effective range. (Left, © Esther Carré; right, Rabax63/ Wikimedia Commons/ CC-BY-SA-4.0)

enterprise. To the ordinary Roman, the invasion of Britannia would be a spectacular feat, which would overcome not simply military opposition, but also Roman superstition and fear of the Oceanus. The concept of a foreign military adventure in order to bolster the prestige of a leader back home is not unfamiliar in today's world.

THE ROMAN PLAN

The invasion of Britannia was a very reasonable gamble for Claudius, who, after all, sorely needed a *iutus triumphus* (legitimate triumph) to secure his position in Rome. The place was so remote from the Mediterranean world that it offered no real threat of retaliation to Rome if the enterprise failed. On the other hand, its association with the earlier (failed?) attempt at conquest by the illustrious Caesar offered the prospect of real glory, if the invasion could somehow be made to succeed. It was a calculated gambit, and, if it came off, Claudius could claim he had out-Caesared Caesar.

Full-scale replica of *lorica segmentata*, Corbridge Type A (Kelten Römer Museum, Manching). The horizontal curved strips of steel encircling the torso were resistant to much heavier blows than the iron rings of *lorica hamata*, and they also afforded the soldier excellent freedom of movement, particularly of the shoulders. However, the multiplicity of copper-alloy buckles, hooks and hinges that allowed this mobility, and the leather fixings between the different plates, were surprisingly frail. The current view is that this type of body armour was first used in about 14 BC, as attested by the frieze on the Arch of Augustus, Susa. Archaeological finds indicate that Corbridge Type B was already in use during the Claudian invasion. This assembly had seven instead of the eight pairs of girdle plates of Corbridge Type A, with hook and loop fastening between girdle and shoulder plates instead of buckled straps. (Wolfgang Sauber/Wikimedia Commons/CC-BY-SA-3.0)

THE BRITANNIC PLAN

Having missed the opportunity to gain a quick victory over the invaders as they came ashore (see below, p. 56), the Britons chose not to meet the Romans in pitched battle, opting instead to engage in indirect actions. The objective now for the Britons was rather straightforward: Disperse and dispatch the Roman invasion force; move or burn all the enemy needs (crops, shelter); round up or slaughter everything edible (cattle, sheep); attack, hinder and disappear. And in this way, the Britons adhered to the time-honoured method for fighting their inter-tribal conflicts. Caesar had faced this indirect style of warfare in 54 BC:

> Even when they did assemble, they refused to come to close quarters with the Romans, but fled to the swamps and forests, hoping to wear out the enemy and force him to sail away again, just as they had done in the time of Iulius Caesar. (Dio 60.19.5)

Reading between the lines, initially the Britons resisting the invasion of AD 43 were planning to employ tactics of a more or less guerrilla nature: Sporadic but spirited skirmishes with isolated units (such as scouts, foragers and the like) and those that strayed too far from the column of march.

THE CAMPAIGN

Unlike the Caesarian adventures, when we have an eyewitness account (however prejudiced) for the events, which in addition can be checked against other contemporary sources such as the correspondences of Cicero, the historical sources for the Claudian invasion are much poorer, and the sequence of events has to be pieced together from a variety of different accounts. There are five short accounts available in the following larger historical accounts: *Roman History* of Cassius Dio (written in the first half of the 3rd century AD), *Agricola* of Tacitus (written in the late 1st century AD), *Divus Claudius* and *Divus Vespasianus* of Suetonius (both written in the early 2nd century AD), as well as a paragraph each in the 4th century AD *Breviarium Historiae Romanae* of Flavius Eutropius (7.13.2–3) and the early 5th century AD *Historiae adversus paganos* of Orosius (7.6.9–10). There are also oddments of information in *Bellum Iudaicum* of Flavius Josephus (late 1st century AD) and *Historiae* of Tacitus (3.44), which relate mainly to Vespasianus' role in the initial conquest. All in all, it is not much to go on.

Eutropius was writing in the second half of the 4th century AD, and he does not always get his facts right when he deals with Britannia. Particularly interesting is his claim that the Orkney Isles were acquired at the time of the Claudian invasion. If this is really true, Tacitus' declaration that his father-in-law, Agricola, was the first to discover and subjugate those islands in AD 83 (*Agr.* 10.4) is thrown into a bad light. This is what Eutropius had to say:

> [Claudius] made war upon Britannia, which no Roman since C[aius] Caesar had visited; and, having reduced it through the agency of Cn[aeus] Sentius and

(Left) Marble votive base (Museo archeologico e d'arte della Maremma, Grosseto) dated AD 45 bearing an inscription (*AE* 2003, 1014) commemorating the Claudian invasion of Britannia. It reads: VOTO [s]VSCEPTO / [p]RO SALVTE ET REDITV ET / VICTORIA BRITANNI/CA TI(beri) CLAVDI CAESA/RIS AVG(usti) GERMANICI / PONT(ificis) MAX(mi) TR(ibuncia) POT(estate) V IMP(eratoris) / X P(atris) P(atriae) CO(n)S(ulis) DES(ignati) IIII / A(ulus) VICIRIVS PROCVLVS / FLAMEN AVG(ustalis) TR(ibunus) MIL(itum) / VICTORIAE BRITANNI/CAE VOTVM SOLVIT. (Right) Marble votive base (Museo archeologico e d'arte della Maremma, Grosseto) dated AD 45 bearing an inscription (AE 2001, 956) saluting Claudius for his victory in Britannia. It reads: EX VOTO SVSCEPTO / [p]RO SALVTE TI(beri) CLAVDI CAESARIS / AVG(usti) F(ilii) BRIT(t)ANNICI / A(ulus) VICIRIVS A(uli) F(ilius) PROCVLVS / TR(ibunus) MIL(itum) FLAMEN [A]VGVSTALIS POSVIT. (Sailko/Wikimedia Commons/CC-BY-SA-3.0)

A[ulus] Plautius, illustrious and noble men, he celebrated a magnificent triumph. (3) Certain islands also, called the Orcades [Orkney Isles], situated in the Oceanus, beyond Britannia, he added to the Roman empire, and gave his son the name of Britannicus. (Eutr. 7.13.2–3)

The same claim with regards to the addition of the Orkney Isles by Claudius to the empire is repeated by Orosius. He also lets on that he had used Suetonius as one of his literary sources, though the latter makes no mention of this in his *Divus Claudius*. This is what Orosius had to say:

In the fourth year of the reign, Claudius had the intention to prove himself to the state as a useful emperor … (10) Therefore he invaded Britannia, which was apparently in unrest, because the refugees had not been returned. There was a crossing onto the island, which nobody either before or after Iulius Caesar had dared to approach. There – in the words of Suetonius Tranquillus – without a battle and bloodshed, he accepted in the shortest span of days the surrender of the larger part of the island. He even added the islands of the Orcades [Orkney Isles] which lie beyond Britannia in the Oceanus to the Roman rule and returned to Rome in the sixth month after his departure. (Oros. 7.6.9–10)

Though the Romans were obviously aware of the Orkney Islands, no signs of occupation have been found, the archaeological evidence indicating that they only traded with the inhabitants.

THE CLAUDIAN CONUNDRUM

Cassius Dio writes briefly of the Claudian invasion, but omits any topographical details except for two references to the river Thames, τὸν Ταμέσαν ποταμὸν (60.20.5, 21.3) and one to Colchester, τὸ Καμουλόδουνον (60.21.4). Aulus Plautius must have landed somewhere. The question, of course, is where?

There are two schools of thought. Supporters of the Chichester (Fishbourne) landing site point to the military structures under the palatial villa at Fishbourne and its early, bright-red polished pottery, namely Arretine ware dated to the reigns of Augustus and Tiberius. Associated with this pottery is a copper-alloy fitting believed to be part of a scabbard of a *gladius*. This leads to the argument that there was a Roman presence in support of a local client king before AD 43. Client kingdoms were a standard Roman practice of frontier policy, and were certainly evident in Britannia throughout the period of Roman occupation.

Reculver looking west by south from a light aircraft at 600ft (183m). The mown, sub-rectangular area of grass around the ruins of the church of Saint Mary the Virgin marks the remaining interior of the 3rd-century AD Saxon Shore fort known as Regulbium (the rest of the fort has disappeared into the sea). A monastery and church were built in AD 669 by Ecgberht, King of Kent (r. AD 664–73), reusing the stone from the old fort, while the remaining twin towers were added in the 12th century. The church was mostly demolished in 1809. (Geoff soper/Wikimedia Commons/ CC-BY-SA-4.0)

Supporters of the Richborough landing site point to the double-ditch, dated by coins and pottery to the reign of Claudius, under the later Saxon Shore fort. Furthermore, in September of 2008 a team of archaeologists from English Heritage unearthed evidence at Richborough of Roman ditches that they believe indicates the Claudian invasion site.

Both sides can point to an impressive natural harbour, the Solent and the Wantsum tidal channel respectively, in their favour. Both camps can point to possible sites for the river crossing (be that at Pulborough over the Arun, at Rochester over the Medway, or any other river proposed), as it is one of the few geographical fixed points. Both end up on the lower Thames and at Colchester, the campaign's ultimate objective.

Richborough Castle, Kent, site of one of the (if not the only) Claudian beachheads. Today, Richborough itself is a small sandy hill rising some 18m above sea level, and sitting some 3km inland. But when the Isle of Thanet was separated from the mainland by the Wantsum tidal channel, Rutupiae, as the Romans called it, overlooked a sheltered tidal lagoon. Here we see the remains of the massive weather-beaten masonry that once formed the north wall of the later Saxon Shore fort. (Ad Meskens/Wikimedia Commons/ CC-BY-SA-4.0)

Those who suggest the landing could have taken place at Chichester point to the fact that it would have given better access to what would later be called Calleva Atrebatum–Silchester, Verica's former seat of power. It is also suggested that Verica and his Roman backers would have received a friendly welcome. But there are a number of problems with this hypothesis. Let us consider each in detail.

First, Calleva Atrebatum–Silchester is some 65km inland. A fully equipped Roman soldier was expected to march 24 Roman miles (35.54km) in five hours, at least in summer time (Veg. *Mil.* 1.9), and be fit enough to construct a marching camp at the end. By this reckoning, therefore, the distance from the coast at Chichester to Calleva Atrebatum–Silchester was the equivalent of two days' loaded march for the invasion army, unimpeded, of course.

Second, the intervening territory had recently come under the control of the Catuvellauni. Besides, did Verica not betray his trust as the leader of his people to a foreign power?

Third, it seems more likely that the restoration of a Britannic client would be a by-product of the invasion, not its primary purpose.

Fourth, in order to reach the Thames, as Cassius Dio describes, the Romans would have to slog their way through the bottomless bogs and tangled forest of the Weald. The Weald, of course, was not impassable; the locals would have used well-known tracks. But this does not make it suitable terrain for a fully laden army. Had Aulus Plautius forced his army through the tortuous terrain of the Weald, he would have surely brought upon himself and his men a catastrophe such as was suffered by Varus and his hapless three legions in AD 9. Even if the Romans bypassed the Weald by skirting it to the west, as has been suggested, this route was a long way from the lower Thames.

Fifth, to sail to Chichester the invasion fleet would have to travel through the passing of three tides, one in its favour and two against; the journey time would have been at least 20 hours, compared with the six-hour journey on one tide to Richborough. A general as experienced as Aulus Plautius would have chosen the shortest invasion route to Britannia from his base in north-west Gaul, which, after all, was the better known crossing and had been since the days of Caesar.

Aerial view of the Isle of Thanet, the north-eastern point of Kent, as seen from the north. The Romans knew the island (as it was then) as Tanatus Insula. At the top right is the former Wantsum tidal channel. In Roman times, the channel, some 3km wide and 9m deep at its widest point, linked Rutupiae–Richborough and Regulbium–Reculver, and was capable of accommodating sea-going vessels. It was used by the Romans as a thoroughfare connecting the Strait of Dover (Oceanus) with the Thames (Tamesis) estuary, thus avoiding the dangerous waters around North Foreland (seen bottom left-hand corner). The continuing strategic importance of the channel is shown by the establishment of two Saxon Shore forts at the aforementioned sites in the 3rd century AD. It was the Saxons who gave it the name Wantsum, to illustrate its decreasing size, for it was being filled with silt from the Thames estuary and the Stour river. Its course is now represented by the rivers Stour and Wantsum. (Lewis Clarke/Wikimedia Commons/CC-BY-SA-2.0)

Sixth, after the mutiny (which we will come to later), it would have been expedient for the restoration of moral and of discipline for the sea crossing to Britannia to be as short as possible.

Having said all that, the viability of the Richborough invasion bridgehead turns on the assumption that the invasion army embarked at Gesoriacum–Boulogne-sur-Mer. The only hint from our literary sources is the statement of Suetonius (*Claud*. 17.2) that Claudius himself, when called upon by Aulus Plautius, sailed for Britannia from Gesoriacum–Boulogne-sur-Mer. Other than that, it was certainly to serve as the chief naval base for the Classis Britannica, and it was used by Iulius Caesar to launch his two expeditions to Britannia. The simple question is: Would Plautius have risked his commander-in-chief landing in Britannia other than at an already established and secured bridgehead? The simple answer is: Not very likely.

As Gerald Grainge (2005) has tightly argued, the Roman invasions of Britain, of which there were four, were largely governed by weather patterns, tidal regimes and seamanship. Another factor to consider, as he rightly points out, is the effects of coastal change. The coastline the Romans left and encountered was significantly different to that of the present day. First, though present-day Calais is much nearer the Kentish coast than Boulogne, and on a clear day the chalk cliffs can often be made out, in AD 43 it was under the sea. Now 40km inland, the location of Saint-Omer was then on the coast of Gaul. Second, the coastline the Romans encountered was more intricate and indented, with longer sand and gravel spits embaying large lagoons. The coastline also extended further out to sea. The Isle of Thanet is thus no longer an island, the Wantsum tidal channel between Reculver and Richborough having long silted up. Likewise, the lagoons between Sandwich and Deal, Romney Marsh and Pevensey Bay, and the former tidal inlet at Dover, no longer exist. Many of these coastal spots were probably under water in the winter, and were a waterlogged, impenetrable waste in the summer.

Given the above, and the fact that the archaeological footprint weighs in its favour, there is a good, if not compelling, case for arguing that Rutupiae–Richborough was the most likely location for the invasion bridgehead in AD 43.

THE INVASION FORCE ASSEMBLES

The invasion force probably assembled around the beginning of April, the seas being too tempestuous to cross before this month; Britannia was virtually cut off from mainland Europe for nigh on half of the year because of the perils of winter navigation. As Vegetius says: 'from three days before the Ides of November [11 November] until six days before the Ides of March [10 March] the seas are closed' (*Mil.* 4.39).

When territory was added to the empire, a garrison had to be put together to serve in its defence. New legions were sometimes raised, but normally these green units were not themselves intended for service in the new province. So when an invasion and permanent occupation of Britannia became a hard possibility under Caius Caligula, two new legions – XV Primigenia and XXII Primigenia – were formed in advance. Their intended role was as replacements for experienced legions earmarked to join the invasion force: Legio XV Primigenia to release Legio XX from Novaesium–Neuss, and Legio XXII Primigenia to release Legio XIIII Gemina from Mogontiacum–Mainz. The invasion force that eventually sailed for Britannia in the summer of AD 43 consisted of *legiones* XX and XIIII Gemina, along with Legio II Augusta, which had been at Argentoratum–Strasbourg (this base was now left vacant), and Legio VIIII Hispana from Siscia–Sisak in Pannonia, which may have accompanied the outgoing *legatus pro praetore*, Aulus Plautius, on his journey to take up his new post as the expeditionary commander (Birley 2005, pp. 17–25).

It must be said, however, that the positive evidence for the participation of these four legions in the invasion is imperfect. Some modern commentators would even go so far as to argue that all of this is mere speculation. The one legion about which there is certainty is II Augusta from Tacitus (*Hist.* 3.44), who also informs us that Vespasianus was its *legatus legionis*. There is also epigraphical evidence for this legion too (*ILS* 2696), more of which later.

The inclusion of Legio XX is implied by its early appearance at Camulodunum–Colchester, as signified by the funerary stele of *centurio* Favonius Facilis, and a further inscription found at Ephesos recording a *praefectus fabrum* who was decorated in the campaign (*AE* 1924, p. 78).

For Legio VIIII Hispana, Lawrence Keppie (1971, p. 155) points our attention to an epigraphic fragment (*CIL* v.7165), recording someone accompanying Claudius to Britannia, and who had *HOSPITIVM CVM LEG V...* – and this could be VIIII Hispana. It had been on continuous operations in Pannonia since being transferred there from Iberia some time in AD 9 – it was there that it gained its honorific title during the Iberian campaigns of Augustus (27–13 BC) – and after AD 43 it no longer appears in the Pannonian records.

There is no direct evidence for Legio XIIII Gemina in the invasion; the earliest evidence for the unit being in Britannia is on two, possibly three, funerary *stelae* (*RIB* 292, 294 and probably 296) from Viroconium Cornoviorum–Wroxeter, which are not likely to be earlier than AD 56. One of these is worth quoting, simply for its down-to-earth witticism at the end of the epitaph:

Chalk cliffs of South Foreland, Kent coast, viewed from the Strait of Dover. In a letter to his friend Atticus, Cicero wrote: 'the approaches to the island are known to be warded with wondrous massy walls' (*Att.* 4.16.7). Clearly, Cicero was referring to what are now known as the White Cliffs of Dover, which stretch for some 13km at the point where Britain is closest to the European mainland. Cicero would have come by this topographical titbit via his younger brother Quintus, who would have seen the 'massy walls' for himself when he accompanied Caesar on his second expedition in 54 BC. (Piotr Kuczynski/ Wikimedia Commons/ CC-BY-SA-4.0)

Funerary stele (Musée archéologique, Strasbourg) of Comnisca, son of Vedillus, a trooper of Ala Gallorum Indiana, recently discovered in the Strasbourg district of Koenigshoffen (2013). This was a Gaulish auxiliary cavalry unit, named after it first commander, Iulius Indus, a noble of the Treveri who helped put down a rebellion of the Treveri and Aedui in AD 21. The inscription (*AE* 2014, 940) reads: COMNISCA / VEDILLI F(ilius) AMBI/AN(us) EQ(ues) ALA / INDIANA TVR/ MA CELTAE AN(norum) / XXV STIP(endiorum) VII H(ic) S(itus) E(st) / HERES EX TEST(amento) FEC(it). Comnisca was stationed in Argentoratum–Strasbourg, dying at the age of 25 after seven years of service. He is depicted in the stock mounted pose, trampling his 'barbarian' foe. (Ctruongngoc/Wikimedia Commons/CC-BY-SA-3.0)

[Titus F]laminius, son of Titus, of the Pollia tribe, from Fa[ventia], 45 years old, with 22 years' service, soldier of Legio XIIII Gemina. I served as a soldier and now here I am. Read this and be more or less lucky in your life. The gods keep you from the wine-grape and water when you enter Tartarus. Live decently while your star grants you time for life. (Campbell 1994, p. 30/*RIB* 292)

It is known for certain that all four legions were present in Britannia during the Boudican rebellion. We can argue, of course, that in the 17 years between the Claudian invasion and the Boudican rebellion, there were numerous opportunities for a further legion to arrive, or for a legion to be switched.

It is possible that there were *vexillationes* from other legions, which was quite usual in large expeditionary forces. These *vexillationes* would either be returned to their bases once the main fighting was over, or some of their members remained as replacements for the losses in the permanent legionary establishment. As far as the Claudian expeditionary force goes, an inscription found in Turin (Augusta Taurinorum) speaks of a *primus pilus* from Legio VIII Augusta named Caius Gavius Silvanus, who was heavily decorated by the commander-in-chief Claudius himself for service in the *bello Britannico*, 'the Britannic war' (*ILS* 2701). It is probably of no coincidence that VIII Augusta was stationed at Poetovio–Ptuj in Pannonia, the same province which supplied VIIII Hispana and whose *legatus pro praetore* was Aulus Plautius. With all this, the belief that part of VIII Augusta had a share in the invasion has been questioned by Keppie (1971). Another inscription refers to an unnamed *militum tribunus* of Legio V Alaudae who received military decorations from Claudius too (*ILS* 974), although it is not entirely clear whether this was for active service in Britannia or in Germania.

We do know of one praetorian cohort, Cohors VIII Praetoria, taking part in the last phase of the campaign. One of its soldiers, Marcus Vettius Valens, was decorated for valour, receiving the *corona aurea*, a simple gold crown, as well as the more common torques, *armillae* and *phalerae* during the *bello Britan(nico)*. He was decorated a second time, though the circumstances of the award are not known. Vettius Valens went on to become the *primus pilus* of Legio XIIII Gemina Martia Victrix during the reign of Nero. In AD 66, following promotion to the equestrian order, Vettius Valens held the post of *tribunus* of Cohors III Praetoria. He reached the pinnacle of a long and successful career by becoming the procurator of Lusitania, a high official with civil and military powers (*AE* 2009, 468).

The associated *auxilia* are even more difficult to identify, since the names of Roman units are very rarely given by the ancient authorities. Once again, we have to rely on inscriptions.

The evidence from two funerary *stelae*, one from Colchester (*RIB* 201, cf. 109) and one from Gloucester (*RIB* 121), gives us Ala I Thracum and Cohors VI Thracum respectively. The latter commemorates Rufus Sita, an *eques*, which suggests the unit was *equitata* not *peditata*. The only other possible invasion auxiliary unit is that on a stone at Cirencester (*RIB* 108), which records the presence of Ala Gallorum Indiana. Still, the recent discovery in Strasbourg of the funerary stele (*AE* 2014, 940) of an *eques* named Comnisca imparts Ala Gallorum Indiana was stationed in Argentoratum–Strasbourg alongside Legio II Augusta. It is not too farfetched to suggest, therefore, the cavalry unit accompanied the legion when it marched west to join the invasion force gathering at Gessoriacum–Boulogne-sur-Mer.

As Aulus Plautius brought with him from Pannonia Legio VIIII Hispana, it is reasonable to suggest that it was accompanied by some of the *auxilia* from that province. However, there is no evidence for more than two *alae* and at the most five *cohortes* raised in Pannonia, and at one time or another serving in Britannia. Moreover, the earliest evidence for one of these units serving in the province is a *diploma* of 19 January AD 103 issued to a retiring *decurio* of Ala I Pannoniorum Tampiana (*CIL* xvi.48). The *diplomata* are bronze 'booklets', each of two plates, representing the personal certified copies of the official record held in Rome with the names of soldiers (auxiliaries in the main) retired from military service with an honourable discharge, along with certain specific benefits they were now awarded, such as the grant of Roman citizenship. They first appear during the reign of Claudius.

Cold feet

To the soldiers crossing the Oceanus in the late spring or early summer of AD 43, the prospect of invading an island believed to be on its periphery must have meant a mixture of panic and promise. These men were part of a formidable army of four veteran legions, three of which were taken from the army of the Rhine frontier (II Augusta from Argentoratum–Strasbourg, XIIII Gemina from Moguntiacum–Mainz, XX from Novaesium–Neuss) and a fourth (VIIII Hispana) all the way from Siscia–Sisak in Pannonia, on the banks of the Danuvius.

This impressive force had been assembled under the overall command of Aulus Plautius Silvanus (*cos.* AD 29), 'a senator of great reputation' (Dio 60.19.1) and recently *legatus pro praetore* (governor) of the turbulent frontier province of Pannonia (Tac. *Ann.* 14.32.6). Under him were, significantly, first-rate legionary commanders. These included the future emperor Titus Flavius Vespasianus, his elder brother Titus Flavius Sabinus and Cnaeus Hosidius Geta. With the auxiliary units, it is probable that the total invasion force was 40,000 in round numbers, not including the naval personnel needed for its transportation and protection, but having assembled at Gessoriacum–Boulogne-sur-Mer, the men refused to embark:

> Thus it came about that Aulus Plautius undertook the campaign, but he had great difficulty in persuading his army to leave Gaul. The soldiers objected to the idea of campaigning outside the limits of the world they knew, and would not obey Plautius until Narcissus, who had been sent by Claudius, mounted Plautius' tribune and attempted to address them. (Dio 60.19.2)

Cassius Dio uses the Greek term τῆς οἰκουμένης, which is best translated as 'the known civilized world'. Even if this was a literary trope of an educated Greek rather than

Colonne de la Grande Armée, Boulogne-sur-Mer, département du Pas-de-Calais. The sea has kept Britain safe from invasion even into the 20th century. There have only been two successful invasions, the Roman and Norman. As Napoléon famously wrote on 2 July 1804 in a communiqué to Vice Admiral Latouche-Tréville, commanding the fleet of Toulon, 'Let us be masters of the Straits for six hours and we shall be masters of the world'. For the planned invasion of Britain of the yet-to-be-crowned emperor, Boulogne was to serve as his principle port of embarkation. (MJJR/Wikimedia Commons/CC-BY-SA-2.5)

factual reality, viewed from the mainland of Europe it was the terror of the open sea which outweighed fears of fighting on the beaches. It appears the hardened and disciplined soldiers of the Roman army were not inclined towards maritime diversions, especially if it meant being crammed onto the pitching deck of a heavily laden transport, wearing full armour and loaded down with all their weapons and war gear. Little wonder, therefore, to find the men hesitating before committing themselves to the will of the immeasurable Oceanus, a fearsome sea to men as yet unaccustomed to the tidal conditions outside of the inner sea – 'Our Sea' – a sea without significant tides.

Tiberius Claudius Narcissus was a Greek freedman, a senior figure in the emperor's household. He is described as *praepositus ab epistulis*, in charge of correspondence. According to Suetonius, Vespasianus 'was indebted to Narcissus for the command of a legion [II Augusta] in Germania' (Vesp. 4.1), thus giving us some indication of the enormous power of this imperial freedman. Still, when he stood upon the commander's tribune to address the mutinous soldiers, Narcissus was probably greeted with angry mutterings. Then someone cried '*Io Saturnalia!*' The Saturnalia was a Roman holiday in the midwinter, an annual festival when slaves swapped roles with their masters for the day. The jibe, obviously, amounted to recognition by one of the soldiers that, however senior, Narcissus was no more than a former slave, and a Greek-speaking one at that. The mood would have lightened once it dawned upon the soldiers that Narcissus was now acting the part of their commander-in-chief. This would have appealed to their grim sense of humour and shamed them into obedience. However, Narcissus no doubt, amidst the merriment, announced more tangible inducements than just appeals to the soldiers' sense of honour and duty.

It is a reasonable speculation that the experienced Aulus Plautius rightly appreciated that the best way of stifling any lingering thoughts of mutiny lay in action. If this was the case, he promptly ordered the invasion army break camp and board the waiting fleet.

CROSSING THE OPEN DEEP

Once the mutinous atmosphere was dispelled and the soldiers had embarked, the invasion fleet, we are told by Cassius Dio, sailed in 'three divisions, so that their landing should not be hindered, as might happen with a single force' (60.19.4). It is not clear whether the landing was at three separate

The Roman beachhead at Richborough

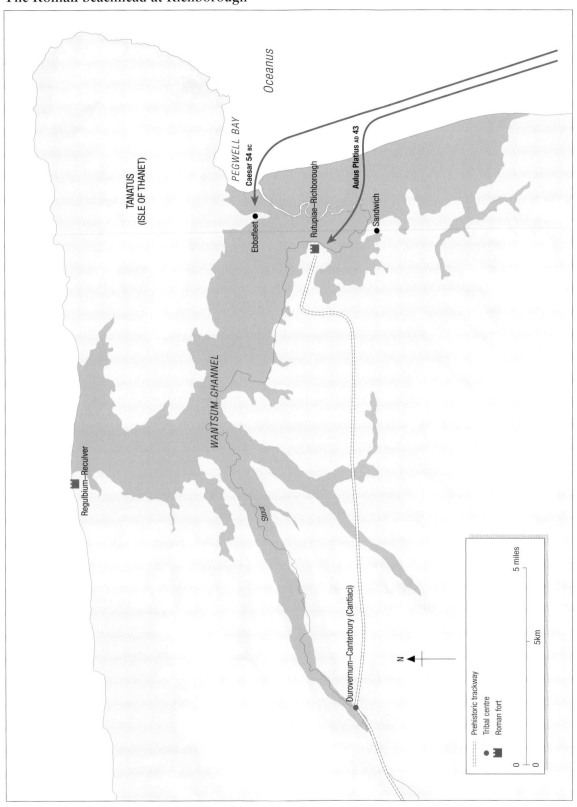

Oceanus

PEGWELL BAY

Caesar 54 BC

Aulus Platius AD 43

TANATUS
(ISLE OF THANET)

Ebbsfleet

Rutupiae–Richborough

Sandwich

WANTSUM CHANNEL

Regulbium–Reculver

Stour

Durovernum–Canterbury (Cantiaci)

N

Prehistoric trackway
Tribal centre
Roman fort

0
0

5km

5 miles

Pilgrims' Way, North Downs, Kent. This was actually a skein of routes rather than a single path, which took pilgrims, following the canonization of Thomas à Becket (martyred 29 December 1170), to Canterbury. Canterbury itself sits on the site of Durovernum Cantiacorum, the principal oppidum of the Cantiaci, while one of the aforementioned routes followed a prehistoric trackway formerly known as the Harroway. This prehistoric trackway traversed for the most part along the south-facing escarpment of the chalk ridge to the south of the Medway. In the whole course of this trackway there was but one serious obstacle, the crossing of the Medway. There were probably three crossings, one of which was by a ford somewhere between Snodland and Halling some 6km above Rochester. (Ethan Doyle White/Wikimedia Commons/ CC-BY-SA-3.0)

North Downs Way near Hollingbourne, Kent. The Harroway, believed to date from before 2000 BC, runs on or parallel to the North Downs Way. The importance of the prehistoric trackways that existed before the Roman occupation of Britannia is that they were routes that missed marshy ground, were not too undulating and remained reasonably dry underfoot in most weathers. Often, the best path closely followed the southern slopes of a chalk ridge, or failing that, along the more exposed summit. The Harroway, which ran from the seaside town of Seaton in Devon to the port of Dover in Kent, is possibly associated with the ancient trade in Atlantic tin, albeit in the manner of continuous short-distance exchange, 'down the line'. (GkgAlf/Wikimedia Commons/ CC-BY-SA-3.0)

beachheads or executed in three waves one after the other, but there was no initial opposition. The reason being, as Cassius Dio clearly implies, the Britons were being fed intelligence by their allies in Gaul regarding the Romans and their intentions, not to mention the unrest amongst the Roman rank and file. So, in the end, the Britons 'had concluded that they were not coming and had not assembled to meet them' (Dio 60.19.5). But come they did.

Rutupiae–Richborough, north-east of Sandwich, was certainly one (if not the only one) of the beachheads, but the Claudian camp known there is too small to have been used by the whole invasion force, even allowing for erosion. Even so, one of the arguments for a single landing site from a purely military point of view must be that no commander worth his salt would have divided his army at the outset of a major military operation, least of all one that hinged upon a seaborne landing. What we do know, however, to secure the bridgehead at Rutupiae–Richborough, the Romans threw up earthwork defences consisting of a pair of parallel ditches that

enclosed a 700m section of the shoreline. This defensive work was in all probability designed to protect the ships of the invasion fleet once they had been hauled onto the beach. The Roman beach itself has been discovered, now lying 2m below the surface and some 3km inland from the present coastline.

THE MARCH INLAND

The route followed by Aulus Plautius in the direction of the Medway is not indicated by Cassius Dio, and can only be a matter of surmise. It has been suggested that it was most probably via Durovernum–Canterbury, where the Stour was fordable. From Durovernum–Canterbury to the Medway, the invasion army could have used the dry, high ground of the long-established route of the Harroway. This was a prehistoric trackway, now known for part of its course as the North Downs Way and the Pilgrims' Way, which passes through the heavily wooded chalk landscape of the southern counties.

From Canterbury the trackway initially strikes south-west before turning westward just north of Ashford. The alternative for the invasion army was to follow closely the line of the future Roman road, Watling Street, to the Medway at what is now the town of Rochester. It is also quite feasible that Aulus Plautius split his command between the two routes.

Despite being longer, the Harroway–North Downs trackway does have its advantages. This prehistoric route has been described as both a ridge walk and a terrace way that follows the chalk escarpment of the North Downs. A good rule of thumb is that the prehistoric trackway usually kept to the lower southern slopes that were less exposed than the upper ridges. In this fashion, it thus avoided the cloggy clay found on lower ground, benefiting from the better drainage of the chalk and flint underfoot.

The distance to be travelled between Rutupiae–Richborough and the Medway was roughly 65km, and there would have been many considerations concerning logistics, particularly if some 40,000 men were involved, not to mention the cavalry mounts and the transport mules too. Unsurprisingly, Cassius Dio is silent upon such mundane matters.

Obverse of an *aureus* (*RIC* I, no. 29) of Tiberius struck at Lugdunum–Lyon, found (1957) in the village of Bredgar, Kent. This coin was part of a hoard of 34 coins that ended with those of Claudius dated AD 41–42. It is postulated that the hoard was buried by a Roman soldier during the Claudian invasion. The inscription reads: TI(berius) CAESAR DIVI AVG(usti) F(ilius) AVGVSTVS. (Colchester Museums/CC-BY-SA-4.0)

Legionaries crossing the Danuvius (Danube) by pontoon bridge, as depicted in a bas-relief on the Column of Marcus Aurelius, Rome. Similar Roman pontoon bridges are depicted on Trajan's Column (First Dacian War, scenes 3/III–4/IV, Second Dacian War, Scene 101/CI). These examples are of a semi-permanent nature, their floating pontoons being heavy wooden boats, while each bridge is equipped with side rails. Simpler forms consisted of a string of barrels, lashed together with a wooden walkway laid across them. (MatthiasKabel/Wikimedia Commons/CC-BY-SA-3.0)

The Roman advance to the Medway and the Thames

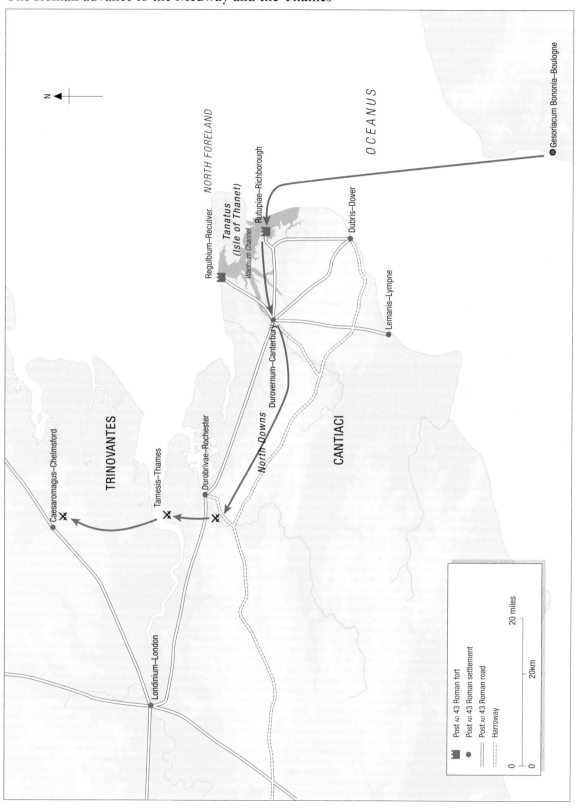

OCEANUS

Gesoriacum Bononia–Boulogne

NORTH FORELAND

Tanatus
(Isle of Thanet)

Wantsum Channel

Rutupiae–Richborough

Regulbium–Reculver

Dubris–Dover

Lemanis–Lympne

Durovernum–Canterbury

North Downs

TRINOVANTES

CANTIACI

Caesaromagus–Chelmsford

Tamesis–Thames

Durobrivae–Rochester

Londinium–London

Post AD 43 Roman fort
Post AD 43 Roman settlement
Post AD 43 Roman road
Harroway

0   20 miles
0   20km

THE MEDWAY

The narrative of Cassius Dio is not only extremely brief, but sketchy by the standards with which we usually have to be content in studying the military history of Rome. Yet it is our sole source for the two riverine battles of the Claudian invasion, and does, on cold reflection, contain four significant nuggets of information with regards to the first of these, the Battle of the Medway.

First, that the Medway encounter lasted two days – a most unusual occurrence in ancient warfare, for few battles lasted more than a day, and these were in fact often decided in no more than a few hours, with one side breaking and running.

Second, on the first day there were two distinct attacks, the first taking the Britons completely by surprise.

Third, the Britons assumed that the Romans would not be able to cross the river without a bridge, which implies the existence of a bridge presumably purposely destroyed beforehand. Alternatively, the Britons expected the Romans to build a bridge before committing themselves to battle. As Cassius Dio himself says in a much later passage: 'Rivers are bridged by the Romans with the greatest ease, since the soldiers are always practising bridge building, which is carried on like any other warlike exercise, on the Ister [Danube], the Rhenos [Rhine], and the Euphrates' (71.3). Certainly, legionaries were quite accustomed to bridging large rivers during the course of a campaign, though the one Caesar's men threw across the Rhine took them ten days to build (Caes. *B Gall.* 4.18.1), while Vegetius talks of bridging a large river 'by driving in piles and boarding over the top, or else, for temporary work, empty barrels may be tied together and timbers placed upon them to provide a passage' (*Mil.* 3.7). The latter structure is obviously meant to be a pontoon bridge, as it is designed for impermanent use. Unlike Caesar's bridge across the Rhenus, the components of this basic pontoon bridge would have been easily transported and quickly assembled. No nails or pegs would be required in its construction; everything would have been speedily lashed together.

Fourth, if this stretch of the Medway needed a bridge, then it is possible that it could not be crossed by wading because of the depth of its water, force of its flow, its steep riverbanks, its treacherously muddy riverbed or, of course, a combination of these factors.

The Medway at the Medway Gap, Snodland, Kent, seen from Blue Bell Hill (186m) on the North Downs looking west over the village of Wouldham, a promising location for the crossing of the river by the Romans during the two-day battle. The Medway rises in Ashurst Forest in the High Weald, and flows northwards through Kent, Maidstone and the chalk escarpment of the North Downs to join the easterly flowing Thames at Sheerness, a total distance of some 113km. The river makes a gap as it cuts north through the ridge south of Maidstone, and a larger one, the Medway Gap, through the North Downs between Maidstone and Rochester towards the Thames. (Courtesy of Helga Brandt)

ROMAN

1. Legio II Augusta
2. Legiones VIIII Hispana, XIIII Gemina, XX
3. Cohortes (Batavorum?) Equitatae
4. Ala Gallorum Indiana

MEDWAY RIVER

TOGODUMNUS/
CARATACUS

EVENTS

1. The Cohortes Equitatae, acting as a diversion, move towards the Roman left and swim across the Medway.

2. Caught unawares, some of the Britannic chariots hurriedly swing towards their left in an attempt to intercept the Roman auxiliaries.

3. In the meantime, Vespasianus leads the Legio II Augusta towards the Roman right, and initiates the crossing of the Medway via the Harroway ford. The legion is supported by the Ala Gallorum Indiana.

4. Seeing the Romans entering the Medway, Britannic war bands rush towards the ford to challenge Legio II Augusta.

5. The Cohortes Equitatae safely reach the west bank, and fall upon the arriving chariots, disabling the horses. With their chariots rendered inoperative, the Britons panic.

6. Vespasianus and the Legio II Augusta face stiff opposition from the arriving war bands, as they fight their way across the ford. Come nightfall, Legio II Augusta digs in on the west bank and awaits the dawn.

BATTLE OF THE MEDWAY – DAY 1

On the first day of the Medway clash, there are two distinct attacks, the first of which takes the Britons completely by surprise. Cassius Dio remarked: 'the barbarians thought the Romans would be unable to cross without a bridge; in consequence they had camped in careless fashion on the far bank' (60.20.2).

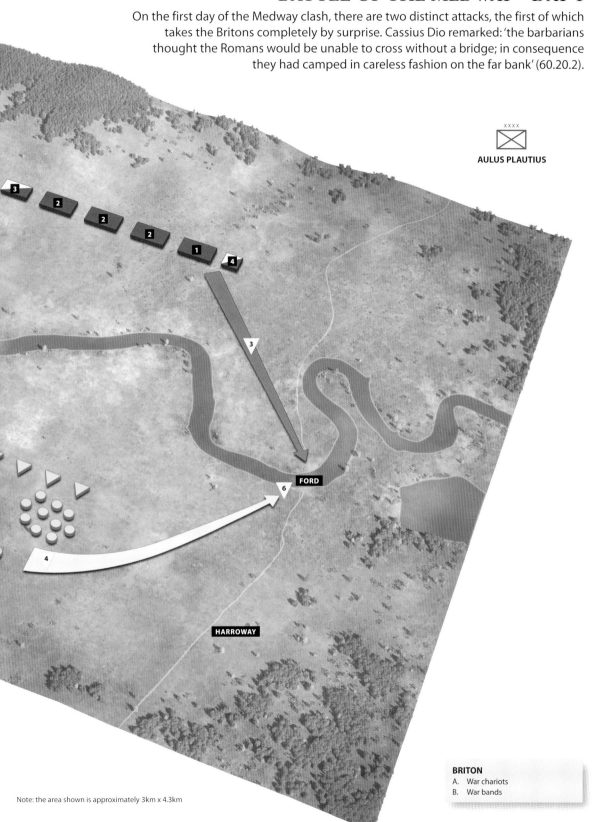

AULUS PLAUTIUS

FORD

HARROWAY

BRITON
A. War chariots
B. War bands

Note: the area shown is approximately 3km x 4.3km

LEGIO II AUGUSTA SPEARHEADS THE ASSAULT ACROSS THE MEDWAY (PP. 62–63)

It is common to most of humankind that, when confronted with actual danger, men and women have less fear than in its contemplation. We can, however, make one exception in favour of the first battle experienced. With this exception it is found the actual dangers of war are always less terrible face to face than on the night before battle. But for those first-timers, enthusiasm and zeal would soon diminish, and their courage would ooze from their fingers' ends when they reflected upon the possibility of being stabbed by soaring spear, or slashed by swinging sword. But that raw moment of combat was all to come as the men of II Augusta entered the swirling, muddy waters of the Medway.

In this scene, we see Vespasianus (**1**) personally leading his men across the Medway. Two burly centurions (**2** and **3**) are acting as the legate's bodyguard. His legion (**4**) are attempting to cross the river by means of a ford found earlier in the day by scouts. The water is knee to thigh high.

The Romans are being challenged by a throng of Britannic warriors (**5**), some of whom have decided to enter the river in a determined attempt to halt the attackers. War horns blare, weapons rattle against shields, roars of defiance carry across the river; the Britons are ready to fight.

The engagement

Cassius Dio describes how Aulus Plautius ordered a detachment of Roman auxiliaries – Κελτοί, 'Keltoi', he calls them – 'who were accustomed to swimming in full equipment across the strongest streams' (60.20.2), to swim the Medway. This they did, unexpectedly, as far as the opposition were concerned, and upon reaching the opposite bank fell upon the horses harnessed to the chariots, surprising the Britons and causing panic. The initial onslaught by the Roman auxiliaries was evidently a discouraging development for the Britons. As Cassius Dio makes clear, 'in the ensuing confusion not even the enemy's mounted men escaped' (60.20.3); that is to say, the chariot warriors, who presumably had dismounted to fight on foot, were neutralized along with their chariots. Following up on this initial advantage, Vespasianus led Legio II Augusta over the river, but despite the enemy's initial disarray was unable to secure a victory. The battle continued throughout the day without reaching a definite conclusion for either side.

Medieval bridge crossing the Medway River at Aylesford, Kent. The village has been suggested as the site of the Battle of the Medway, but there is no direct evidence to support the claim. Though Cassius Dio does hint to the possible existence of a bridge, the two-day contested crossing of the river was more likely closer to the future town of Rochester, some 13km downstream from Aylesford. (Lynbarn/Wikimedia Commons/Public Domain)

On the second day, Aulus Plautius launched a surprise attack, which was headed by Hosidius Geta. He and his legion probably crossed the Medway at the same location as that used by Vespasianus the previous day, moving through his position to attack northwards along the west bank of the river. Hosidius Geta almost fell into enemy hands during the fierce fighting that ensued. However, the legate's men rallied around him, and the opposition was eventually overcome, with the bulk of the Britannic force taking to its heels. The part Hosidius Geta played was obviously decisive, for in due course he would be awarded *ornamenta triumphalia*, an honour of unusual merit for one who had yet to gain the consulship.

The fact that the encounter lasted for two days strongly suggests that it was hard-fought and far from decisive with regards to its outcome. Even though the Romans secured a crossing of the Medway, they failed to inflict a crippling blow on the Britons. As a consequence, the Britons were far from finished as a fighting force at this point.

The Medway at Rochester, the lowest bridging point of the river. There is no clear evidence for a bridge at what is now the town of Rochester before the Roman occupation. As for a possible ford, the river was probably too wide and far too tidal at this point. After the Claudian invasion, this was the site of Durobrivae ('the fort at the bridge'), which controlled the important dry crossing over the Medway by the Roman road known by Chaucer's time as Watling Street, the prehistoric grassy trackway paved by the Romans soon after the invasion. A bridge of one kind or another existed here from then on. (Clem Rutter/Wikimedia Commons/ CC-BY-SA-3.0)

ROMAN
1. Legio II Augusta
2. Legiones VIIII Hispana, XIIII Gemina, XX
3. Cohortes (Batavorum?) Equitatae
4. Ala Gallorum Indiana

MEDWAY RIVER

2

3

B

A

N

TOGODUMNUS/ CARATACUS

EVENTS

1. Vespasianus and the Legio II Augusta remain in their overnight position, holding the west end of the Harroway ford.

2. The Cohortes Equitatae act as a blocking force north of the enemy position. Britannic war bands and war chariots shadow the auxiliaries.

3. One of the three remaining legions (VIIII Hispana, XIIII Gemina, or XX), led by Hosidius Geta, moves towards the Harroway ford. It passes through Vespasianus' position, swings north along the west bank of the Medway and launches an attack.

4. The fighting between Britons and Romans is fierce. Hosidius Geta is almost taken, but his men rally around him, and renew their efforts against the war bands.

5. Eventually, Togodumnus and Caratacus realize all is up, and quit the battlefield with their surviving war bands and war chariots. Aulus Plautius holds his position along the Medway.

BATTLE OF THE MEDWAY – DAY 2

On the second day, Hosidius Geta leads an attack northward along the west bank of the river. Although the Romans secure a crossing of the Medway, they fail to land a crippling blow on the Britons.

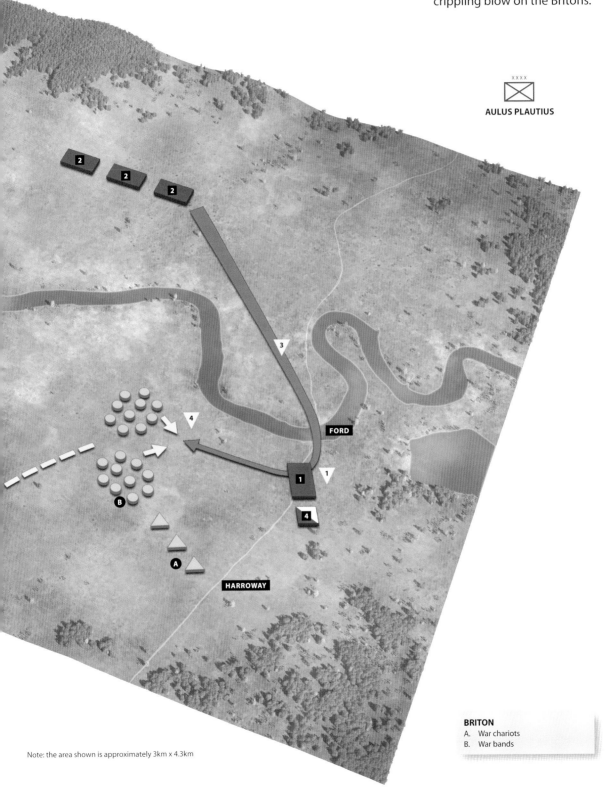

AULUS PLAUTIUS

FORD

HARROWAY

BRITON
A. War chariots
B. War bands

Note: the area shown is approximately 3km x 4.3km

Crossing the Medway

As far as one can tell, Cassius Dio twice mentions the Keltoi, and they alone, because of their exceptional aquatic abilities. Vegetius, writing in the late 4th century AD but looking back to the army of the early principate, says that all legionary recruits 'without exception should in the summer months learn the art of swimming, for rivers are not always crossed by bridges' (*Mil.* 1.10). He repeats his advice when offering a list of recommendations for the continuous and constant training of soldiers, whether they are legionaries or auxiliaries, saying 'that they should very frequently be … swimming in the sea or rivers' (ibid. 2.23, cf. 3.4). However, this drill was not done in full fighting equipment.

It is possible that when the legionaries performed the crossing of the Medway, as surely they must have done, they did so by stacking their arms and armour upon their *scuta*, which they then pushed in front of themselves as they swam across the river. The *scutum*, after all, was protected from the elements when off parade or out of battle by means of an oiled-leather cover; the three layers of plywood used in its construction would have doubled in weight when wet. Then again, there is a scene on Trajan's Column (First Dacian War, Scene 26/XXVI) which depicts legionaries in full fighting order wading across a river. Interestingly enough, one legionary is depicted stripped to the waist with his war gear stacked on his *scutum*, holding it high above his head as he fords a river. If the last scenario is the version of events that came to pass at the Medway, however, it means we have to assume that the legionaries would not have been in a condition to mount an immediate assault on reaching the opposite, enemy-held riverbank. Unfortunately, Cassius Dio does not impart how the legionaries actually crossed.

It is possible, on the other hand, that the legionaries made the crossing of the Medway by way of a ford. No doubt with local help, Roman scouts could have found one, if one existed, of course. This being the case, there is then an argument to be made that Vespasianus led his legion, II Augusta, over the ford that once carried the Harroway–North Downs trackway between Snodland and Burham Court. This is, of course, no more than speculation.

THE THAMES

For the sequel to the Medway battle, Cassius Dio says the next encounter was fought τὸν Ταμέσαν ποταμὸν, 'on the river Thames', the Britons having fallen back 'at a point near where it enters the sea, and at high tide forms a pool' (60.20.5). This would rule out any point above what is now Gravesend and would seem to place it nearer Lower Hope Point, opposite East Tilbury, at 53km east of London Bridge, where the estuary starts to broaden out.

One thing is quite clear: The river has changed dramatically over the centuries, with marshy land and soft natural banks replaced by hard embankments built ever outwards, pinching and narrowing the Thames. Today, the Thames is a tidal canal, restricted to a width in central London of some 250m between solid river walls on both banks. While today there is a strong current with tidal range of 7m on the spring tides and 5.5m on the neap tides, before it was tamed, the Thames was a broad sinuous river with a tidal range of just 3m.

To simplify a complex story: Scientific studies of the Roman Thames have demonstrated its width, depth, salinity and tidal range have all changed markedly since the mid-1st century AD. The evidence of diatoms (unicellular microalgae sensitive to changes in water salinity) suggests the river's tidal head lay upstream of Westminster in the Middle/Late Bronze Age, though by the Roman period it seems as though the tidal head had receded to a point closer to the City. So it seems that the river's tidal head – the point where fresh water meets the incoming sea – has shifted over time.

As a result, the river was much wider and shallower, and probably flowed in a number of different channels. In addition, the difference between the riparian topography at low tide and high tide was particularly dramatic on the south bank. Here, at low tide, the river retreated to reveal an inhospitable expanse of marshes and mudflats, in contrast to the steeply rising dry hillside on the north bank. That is the Thames the Roman soldiers saw in the summer of AD 43.

The engagement

Returning to Cassius Dio and his brief account of the Thames battle, he tells us that the Britons 'crossed over easily because they knew where to find firm ground and an easy passage' (60.20.5). In other words, there were locals among their number who knew the firm and fordable places and the vagaries of the tides. The Romans, however, in attempting to give chase, were not so fortunate.

The Medway Monument, the hamlet of Burham Court, south of Rochester, Kent. The stone was raised in March 1998 on the east bank of the Medway opposite Snodland church to commemorate the crossing of the river by the Roman invasion force in AD 43. The inscription (now badly weathered) reads: 'This stone commemorates the battle of the Medway in AD 43 when a Roman army crossed the river and defeated the British [sic] tribes under Caratacus.' There was once a ferry across the Medway at Snodland, used by Hilaire Belloc (1870–1953): he claimed the river bottom at the crossing had 'been artificially hardened' (1911: 251). In 2005, the weather forecaster of BBC South East, Kaddy Lee-Preston, with the help of the Water Safety Unit of the Kent Fire and Rescue Service, waded across the Medway at Snodland. At this point, Legio II Augusta perhaps crossed the river on the first day of the battle. (Courtesy of Helga Brandt)

As Charles Dickens once said of the Hoo Peninsula, the finger of land that separates the estuaries of the Thames and the Medway, 'A most beastly place. Mudbank, mist, swamp, and work; work, swamp, mist, and mudbank' (*Great Expectations*, ch. 28). Cassius Dio continues his account, saying:

> [The] Keltoi swam across again and some others got over by a bridge a little way up-stream, after which they assailed the barbarians from several sides at once and cut down many of them. In pursuing the remainder incautiously, they got into swamps from which it was difficult to make their way out, and so lost a number of men. (Dio 60.20.6)

Having put the Britons to flight yet again, it is probable that the resistance host, mostly levied from farmsteads and settlements, melted back into the countryside, leaving the kings and chieftains with only their personal war bands and the chariots.

Crossing the Thames

Caesar says 'the river Tamesis [Thames] … can only be crossed at a single spot, on foot, and then with difficulty' (*B Gall.* 5.18.1). During his second expedition in 54 BC, Caesar had to fight his way through an opposed crossing of the river at a fortified ford somewhere in what is now the Greater London area. Bede, writing close to eight centuries after Caesar, claims that the sharpened stakes referred to by him were still visible in his day, 'each of them, on inspection, is seen to be about the thickness of a man's thigh encased in lead and fixed immovably in the river bed' (*Historia ecclesiastica gentis Anglorum* 1.2). But there is no evidence that these were put there by the Britons confronting Caesar that day.

The area around Higham Marshes to the east of Gravesend was once a patchwork of mudflats and salt marshes cut up by meandering tidal sub-channels that flowed into the main channel of the Thames. There were similar mudflats and salt marshes on the northern bank of the Thames at East Tilbury, which could have been more formidable obstacles than the river itself. Since the 13th century, the regime of the Thames has been transformed by the enclosure of the mudflats and salt marshes behind seawalls that have turned them into economically useful pastures protected from tidal inundation (Thornhill 1976, p. 121). The Thames was thus reduced to a single tidal channel.

Amphibious auxilia

It is believed that the subsequent attachment of eight *cohortes* of Batavi to Legio XIIII Gemina suggests that they may have accompanied this legion from the Rhine

The Thames at Tilbury Fort river battery, on the Essex side of the river. Because of human activity and interference in the natural order of things, modern rivers in south-east England are narrower, deeper and flow faster than their prehistoric counterparts. The parameters, therefore, of today's Thames cannot be retrofitted to the Thames of the summer of AD 43. Indeed, the Thames was once very different to what it is today, and the broad reaches of the river below Tilbury and Gravesend did not exist in AD 43. At low tide, therefore, the Romans would have seen a vista of mudflats, sand banks and salt marshes, through which meandered many small streams, with the edges of the river marshy and tree-lined. (Mark.murphy/Wikimedia Commons/CC-BY-SA-3.0)

Aerial view of the Thames at Cliffe Fort, near the village of Cliffe, on the Hoo Peninsula, Kent. This is a disused artillery fort built 1861–70 to guard the entrance to the Thames from seaborne attack. There is sufficient evidence of a crossing point by ferry in the medieval period from Higham on the Kent shore to Coalhouse Point, East Tilbury, on the Essex side of the river. It is the only known ancient ferry across the Thames below Gravesend, which at that time was the usual method of intercourse between the two counties. (Cgfletch/Wikimedia Commons/CC BY-SA 4.0)

frontier when it left to take part in the Claudian invasion (Hassall 1970; Roymans 2004, p. 223). It is known that during the Boudican rebellion, they were definitely attached to Legio XIIII Gemina, and indeed were to depart Britannia with the legion sometime in AD 66 as part of an expedition to the Caucasus that was planned by Nero, which never materialized because of his erratic temperament and subsequent suicide in AD 68 (Tac. *Hist.* 1.6.4, 2.27.2, 4.15.1). Whether or not we can positively identify, as some scholars do, the Batavi with what Cassius Dio calls the Keltoi is another matter entirely. He writes that, on two occasions, the aquatic abilities of said Keltoi gave the invasion army an added advantage in the two assault river crossings it fought that summer.

I suppose there is a scholarly soft spot for the Batavi. After all, unlike other *auxilia* outfits, they do feature an inordinate number of times in our ancient literary and epigraphical sources. Perhaps this is not surprising, if you consider Tacitus informing us that unlike other conquered people, the Batavi paid no taxes to Rome, but 'reserved for battle, they are like weapons and armour, only to be used in war' (*Ger.* 29.1). It is from Tacitus too (*Hist.* 1.59.1, 2.27.2, 2.66.2, 4.12.3, 4.15.1) that we hear of a number of *cohortes* of Batavi serving in Britannia (in 1.59.1 he puts the figure at eight), which would be their arena up until AD 66.

The Batavi lived on an island in the lower Rhenus, in what is now the Rhine–Maas delta, a relatively small place with a total population that has been calculated at no more than 35,000 souls. When you consider there were some 5,000 battle-ready warriors of military age from the tiny region of Batavia serving Rome at any one time, then it would appear that at least one son from every family left home to soldier for the emperor and became permanent immigrants (Roymans 2004, p. 208).

But having said all this, the Batavi, as Tacitus himself explains, 'were once a tribe of the Chatti, and on account of a rising at home, they crossed the river [Rhenus] for those lands which were to make them part of the

THE KELTOI SWIM THE THAMES UNDER FIRE (PP. 72–73)

The sling is believed to have been far more common as a projectile weapon than the bow both in Iron Age Britain and on the Continent. Several possible reasons for this popularity of the sling over the bow include ease of manufacture (less components, inexpensive); ammunition was far easier to obtain (suitable sling stones were frequently from rivers); it was a weapon of choice for juveniles (hunting small game, protecting livestock); and a lack of archery culture in Iron Age Celtic society.

In this scene, Roman auxiliaries from a *cohors equitata* (**1**) are crossing the Thames. The troopers swim beside their horses, each with a foot soldier in tow. Both horse and foot are wearing their body armour (**2**), but helmets, weapons and shields (**3**) are secured to the horses. Waiting on the north riverbank are a cloud of Britannic slingers (**4**, mainly young men), while behind them chariots wait to engage (**5**). As they make their way across the river, the auxiliaries, lacking shield and helmet, suffer losses from a constant shower of incoming sling stones.

Roman empire' (*Ger.* 29.1). Tacitus does not say when they migrated from Germania Magna, though Caesar hints the Batavi had already arrived in his day:

> The Mosa (Meuse) rises from the Vosges mountains (monte Vosego), which is in the territory of the Lingones; and having received a branch of the Rhenus (Rhine), which is called the Vacalas (Waal), forms the island of the Batavi (*insulam efficit Batavorum*), and not more than eighty [Roman] miles from it flows into the Oceanus. (Caes. *B Gall.* 4.10.1)

This particular passage is generally regarded as a later interpolation and most scholars believe that the Batavi split from the Germanic Chatti on the upper Visurgis (Weser) some time after Caesar's conquest of Gaul (51 BC) and before the start of Drusus' incursions into Germania Magna (15 BC). Whenever it occurred, the Batavi were not Keltoi but Germani.

Of course, the Batavi were renowned for their ability to swim large rivers in full battle gear, and then immediately take up battle again, a skill they had first exhibited in the campaign of Germanicus against the Cherusci led by Arminius in attempting to cross the Amisius (Ems), and were to repeat in their crossing of the Padus (Po) near Cremona and the Rhenus (Rhine) rivers during the anarchy of AD 69 (Tac. *Ann.* 2.8, *Hist.* 2.17, 4.12.3, cf. 5.15.1). This attribute is expressed most clearly by Tacitus:

> In the home country, [the Batavi] also had a picked cavalry force specially trained for amphibious operations. These men were capable of swimming the Rhenus while keeping hold of their arms, and maintaining perfect formation. (Tac. *Hist.* 4.12.3)

We should note here that it is Batavi horsemen, not foot, swimming the Rhenus, and at a much later date – AD 118 – Batavian horsemen perform the same feat when they swim the Ister (Danube), albeit during a military pageant in front of the emperor, Hadrianus (Dio 69.9.6, cf. *CIL* iii.3676/*ILS* 2558). Archaeological evidence by way of equine skeletons found in graves certainly suggests a strong equestrian preoccupation with the Batavi. Though the horsemen mentioned by Tacitus probably belonged to the prestigious unit Ala I Batavorum, those mentioned by Cassius Dio were the mounted arm of Cohors III Batavorum Milliaria Equitata. At this date, there were two such *cohortes equitatae* furnished by the Batavi, the other being Cohors I Batavorum Quingenaria Equitata. When they first became *equitatae* units is debatable.

River crossings in general are a dangerous endeavour, even under peacetime conditions, and perhaps it is Vegetius who gives us some insight into how this feat of swimming large rivers fully laden was achieved:

> [The] cavalry are accustomed to take off their accoutrements and make fascines from dry reeds and sedge and place them upon cuirasses and arms, so as not to get them wet. They and their horses swim across, drawing on reins the fascines that they have tied to themselves. (Veg. *Mil.* 3.7)

This brings us to a passage of Tacitus in which he describes an amphibious assault on the island of Mona–Anglesey. The assembled islanders were taken

CLAUDIUS ARRIVES IN BRITANNIA AMID POMP AND CIRCUMSTANCE (PP. 76–77)

Despite his physical disabilities and discerning eccentricities, Claudius was nobody's fool, though of all the family only Augustus himself evidently recognized this. Claudius was an avid reader, wrote numerous histories and literary works and was easily the most learned of the Iulio-Claudian dynasty. Few knew this, of course, for most dismissed him as weak-minded. Robert Graves' brilliant fictional characterization of Claudius in *I, Claudius* and *Claudius the God* as an essentially benign man with a razor-sharp intellect has tended to dominate the wider public's view of the emperor. Close scrutiny of the literary sources, however, reveals a somewhat different kind of man. In addition to his scholarly and cautious nature, he had a cruel streak, as suggested by his addiction to gladiatorial games and his predilection for watching executions (Suet. *Claud*. 34). Worse, he drank and gambled too much.

In this scene, Claudius (**1**) is riding atop an Indian elephant (**2**, *Elephas maximus*), with its telltale bulging forehead, small ears and tusks (though for the emperor's safety, they have been removed), and arched back. It carries a *turres* (**3**) and is controlled by an Indian mahout (**4**) armed with a sharpened goad with a pointed hook. Beside the emperor is Aulus Plautius (**5**), the commander of the invasion army. Behind them is the emperor's *lictor* (**6**).

Escorting the elephant is a cohort of Praetorians (**7**) under the Praetorian prefect Rufrius Pollio (**8**). Would it be wide of the mark to imagine Claudius using a domesticated stately elephant for a ceremonial ride to enter Camulodunum–Colchester? As an avid antiquarian, Claudius was well aware of the fact that war elephants had been a terrifying (if uncontrollable at times) feature of Hellenistic and Punic armies. He would also have been familiar with the spectacular campaigns of Hannibal in Italy, and the possibility that this great general had once ridden an Indian elephant called Surus. We shall never know for sure, but we may borrow that line from Graves where he has Claudius recall: 'I travelled on elephant-back like an Indian prince' (*Claudius the God*, ch. 20).

Members of the Praetorian Guard, bas-relief (Musée du Louvre-Lens, Lens, inv. LL 398) from the Arch of Claudius erected in AD 51 in honour of the successful invasion of Britannia eight years earlier. After his undignified elevation to the purple with the help of the powerful Praetorian Guard, we should not be surprised to find the Praetorians celebrated on Claudius' triumphal arch. As Suetonius puts it, Claudius became emperor *mirabili casu*, 'by an astonishing accident' (*Claud.* 10.1). Inscriptions reveal that he took them and their commander Rufrius Pollio with him to witness the finale of his invasion of Britannia. (Carole Raddato/Wikimedia Commons/ CC-BY-SA-2.0)

completely by surprise, as they were only expecting an assault by boats. Tacitus explains how Agricola outwitted the Britons:

> He picked a body of native auxiliaries who knew the fords, and had that facility in swimming which belongs to their nation, and by means of which they can control simultaneously their own movements, their weapons and horses. (Tac. *Agr.* 18.5)

Interestingly enough, in this passage Tacitus refers to the horsemen as 'native auxiliaries', *auxiliarium*, and not as Batavi.

CLAUDIUS TRIUMPHANT

According to Cassius Dio, because of the difficulties he had experienced at the Thames and the strength of the Britannic opposition, Aulus Plautius 'became afraid, and instead of advancing any farther, proceeded to guard what he had already won, and sent for Claudius' (60.21.1). It is somewhat difficult to imagine the experienced Plautius losing his nerve. I mention this because, in my opinion, fear of the opposition is not the reason why Plautius dug in along the river. It does seem more likely that our general was following a prearranged command; that is, once the Thames was reached, consolidate and send for the commander-in-chief. In any case, one thing is for certain: Claudius needed to be present in person if he was going to earn that bona fide triumph he so desired.

Suetonius does his utmost to play down this personal appearance of Claudius, describing it as 'of no great importance' (*Claud.* 17.1). Suetonius, by the way, had a flair for gossip, and knew how to report it with great dexterity. Yet it does seem clear from the account of Cassius Dio (60.16.7) that Claudius had arranged with Aulus Plautius that he should be summoned to appear so as to receive the capitulation of numerous Britannic tribes. The relevant passages in the *Annales* of Tacitus, the most important commentator on the Iulio-Claudian period, are lost, but we do know that he measured emperors by their military achievements, which were celebrated through the devices of triumphs and the adoption of military titles by the emperors. We do know also that in public images, imperial military responsibilities played a significant role, and the emperor was commonly depicted wearing military dress on statues, bas-reliefs, triumphal arches and coins, often as a conquering hero or a dignified but firm military leader. Moreover, every emperor was personally associated with his troops – as paymaster, comrade and benefactor – and sought to demonstrate that he was a worthy and courageous fellow-soldier, deserving of their complete loyalty. Claudius currently had the steadfast loyalty of the Praetorian Guard, but as for the loyalty of the rest of the army, that was still a matter of some doubt.

Not surprising, therefore, to find a vulnerable Claudius wanting to earn his triumph, not just the empty title, but as we have just mentioned, one that required his personal participation in the campaign. The triumph, now the prerogative of the emperor and his family, was a splendid public occasion, which involved senators, the people and soldiers, and highlighted the emperor's personal military glory. For his triumph, Claudius was to order provincial governors to Rome specifically to witness it (Suet. *Claud*. 17.3).

Cassius Dio provides some details of Claudius' progress to Britannia. Included in the emperor's entourage were not only men of the highest social standing, but an unspecified number of cohorts from the Praetorian Guard, commanded by Rufrius Pollio, one of Claudius' Praetorian prefects (Dio 60.23.2), and some elephants. It does seem likely that the elephants would already have been assembled at Gesoriacum–Boulogne-sur-Mer awaiting the summons of Aulus Plautius. Cassius Dio lends support to this notion when he says 'considerable equipment, including elephants, had already been assembled as reinforcements' (60.21.2).

As for the emperor's senatorial travelling companions, these apparently included the following: Lucius Iunius Silanus Torquatus, then engaged to Claudius' daughter Claudia Octavia (Suet. *Claud*. 24.3, Dio 60.21.5); Marcus Licinius Crassus Frugi (*cos*. AD 27), and his son Cnaeus Pompeius Magnus, son-in-law of Claudius (Suet. *Claud*. 17.3, 27.2; Dio 60.5.7, 60.21.5); Tiberius Plautius Silvanus Aelianus, relative of Aulus Plautius and former in-law of Claudius (*AE* 1956, 208); Cnaeus Sentius Saturninus, one of the two consuls, who had argued for the reinstatement of the Republic after Caligula's murder (Eutr. 7.13.2–3); and Marcus Vinicius (*cos*. AD 30), Caligula's brother-in-law, who had been discussed as a possible candidate for emperor at the same occasion (Joseph. *Ant. Iud.* 19.102 [251]). Other possible members of the entourage included: Lucius Sulpicius Galba, the future emperor, because of whose illness Claudius seemingly postponed the invasion (Suet. *Galb.* 7.1); Decimus Valerius Asiaticus (*suff. cos.* AD 35), a possible accomplice in Caligula's murder (Tac. *Ann.* 11.1); Lucius Coiedius Candidus, Claudius' *quaestor* (*CIL* xi.6163); and Iulius Planta (*ILS* 206).

The emperor was undoubtedly acting on the age-old adage that you should keep your friends close and your enemies closer. Claudius had survived an attempted coup d'état the year before, and including other potential imperial candidates or members of the Senate with known republican convictions would thus have been a wise precaution.

Normally, when an emperor went on campaign, he was in personal charge of every aspect of military life, though of course depending on his experience, he would take advice from his commanders. We can argue, of course, that it is hard to believe that during his short visit to Britannia, Claudius made much difference to the plans already worked out by Aulus Plautius, the emperor's chosen commander on the ground. But that was not the point of Claudius' participation. The huge dedicatory inscription from his (lost) triumphal arch declares, after reciting the titles of the emperor, that 'he received the surrender of 11 kings [reges] of the Britons who had been defeated without any loss of honour [sine ulla iactura], and was the first to bring northern barbarian peoples from across the Oceanus under the sway of the Roman people' (AE 2004, 38).

The phase sine ulla iactura is a somewhat archaic, and was probably selected by Claudius in the sense used by Caesar not in describing losses in battle (as per many translations), but without any loss of honour by Rome. If the new emperor needed a quick political fix to secure his throne and establish himself as a suitable emperor, then this was the solution. As well as his triumph, the Senate would vote Claudius the title Britannicus, which he did not use, but instead bestowed to his son (Dio 60.22.1); the emperor had succeeded in the eyes of Rome where even the brilliant Caesar had failed. By the close of his reign, Claudius would have been hailed as imperator no fewer than 27 times (e.g. ILS 218), more than any emperor until Constantinus I.

VESPASIANUS GOES WEST

In late AD 43 or early in the following year, Aulus Plautius sent Vespasianus westward to secure the south-western flank of the Roman gains. He succeeded, for in the words of Suetonius 'he fought 30 battles, subjugated two warlike tribes [validissimae gentes], and captured more than 20 oppida, besides the entire insular Vectis' (Vesp. 4.1) – Vectis being the Isle of Wight. It seems certain that one of the 'warlike tribes' was the Durotriges, whose territory encompassed what is now the county of Dorset. For the second warlike tribe, it is possible Vespasianus defeated the Dumnonii, who inhabited a territory corresponding to the later counties of Devon and Cornwall. We know that, at some point, Legio II Augusta had its base in Isca Dumnoniorum–Exeter, probably from AD 55 onwards, and from the Flavian period onwards, it was based at Isca Silurum–Caerleon, where it was recorded in AD 253–59 (RIB 334).

This was a grim and hard-fought campaign that took one-quarter of Plautius' army of occupation and the Classis Britannica, which supported the effort from the sea. If, as is just possible, his later wartime actions are anything to go by, Vespasianus' personal courage and leadership in this campaign would have set the appropriate example to the men of his command. Suetonius, for instance, tells us that in Iudaea, during 'the assault on one enemy fortress he was wounded on the knee by a stone and caught several arrows on his shield' (Vesp. 4.6). Likewise, Flavius Josephus, recalling the same war against the Jewish rebels, reports that 'when Vespasianus had positioned his archers, slingers and the whole of his artillery [omnemque iaculatorum multitudi nem adhibitam] and ordered them to shoot at the

Fragment of the huge dedicatory inscription (*AE* 2004, 38), which represents about a quarter to a third of a very formulaic text, from the Arch of Claudius erected in AD 51 on Via Lata (now the Corso) built into the wall in the courtyard of the Palazzo dei Conservatori, Musei Capitolini, Rome. Erected to celebrate the conquest of Britannia, the triumphal arch has not survived, and it is only known by some of its fragments. It appears on the reverse of gold *aurei*, where it is shown surmounted by a statue of Claudius on horseback between two trophies and with an architrave inscribed with the legend DE BRITANN(IS). For Claudius, the invasion was a success, providing him with military prestige he desperately needed, and, naturally, he exploited it to the full. (Jenni Ahonen/Wikimedia Commons/CC-BY-SA-4.0)

Jews, he himself advanced with the infantry up the slope to the spot where the defensive war was weak' (*B Iud.* 3.7.5 [151]). In other words, Vespasianus led his men from the front.

Publius Ancius Maximus, previously the *primus pilus* of Legio XII Fulminata, now *praefectus castrorum*, was decorated by Claudius himself with the *corona muralis* for his gallant actions during the *bellum Britannic(um)*, 'the Britannic war' (*ILS* 2696). This military decoration was a headpiece of gold indented and embattled, and was bestowed upon the soldier who first mounted the wall of a besieged town, city or fortress. By implication, therefore, Ancius Maximus was involved in an action that contributed to the capture of one of the 20 *oppida* taken by his legion.

The finds of two wooden gateposts of the annex of the legionary fortress of Alchester, for which dendrochronology gives both of them felling dates of between October AD 44 and March AD 45, together with a funerary stele of Lucius Valerius Geminus, a veteran of Legio II Augusta, allow us to suggest Alchester as one of the first bases of this legion (Sauer 2001, 2005). The text of the inscription reads:

DIS MANIBVS / L(ucius) Val(erius) L(uci filius) POL(lia tribu) GEMI/NVS FOR(o) GERM(anorum) / VET(eranus) LEG(ionis) [I]I AVG(ustae) / AN(norum) L. H(ic) S(itus) E(st) / HE(res) C(uravit) / E(x) T(estamento)

The formula *H S E* (*hic situs est* – lies here) unmistakably dates this funerary stele to the 1st century AD. Forum Germanorum was a one-horse frontier town at the foot of the Alps in north-west Italy in what is today the Piedmont region, which was once part of Gallia Cisalpina.

It seems Lucius Valerius may not have had much reason to make the journey to his place of birth, for the veteran died, aged 50-something, before

Campaigns under Aulus Plautius

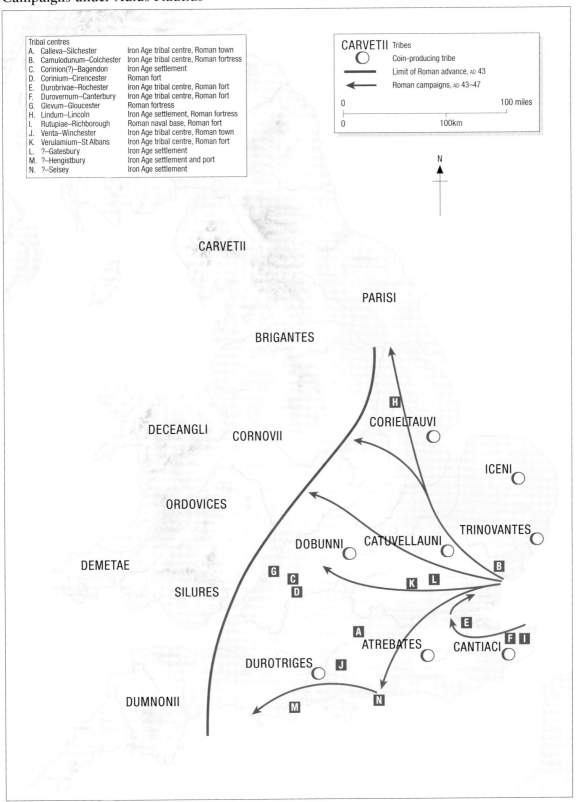

Tribal centres

A.	Calleva–Silchester	Iron Age tribal centre, Roman town
B.	Camulodunum–Colchester	Iron Age tribal centre, Roman fortress
C.	Corinion(?)–Bagendon	Iron Age settlement
D.	Corinium–Cirencester	Roman fort
E.	Durobrivae–Rochester	Iron Age tribal centre, Roman fort
F.	Durovernum–Canterbury	Iron Age tribal centre, Roman fort
G.	Glevum–Gloucester	Roman fortress
H.	Lindum–Lincoln	Iron Age settlement, Roman fortress
I.	Rutupiae–Richborough	Roman naval base, Roman fort
J.	Venta–Winchester	Iron Age tribal centre, Roman town
K.	Verulamium–St Albans	Iron Age tribal centre, Roman fort
L.	?–Gatesbury	Iron Age settlement
M.	?–Hengistbury	Iron Age settlement and port
N.	?–Selsey	Iron Age settlement

CARVETII Tribes

Coin-producing tribe

Limit of Roman advance, AD 43

Roman campaigns, AD 43–47

0   100 miles

0   100km

N

CARVETII

PARISI

BRIGANTES

DECEANGLI   CORNOVII

CORIELTAUVI

ICENI

ORDOVICES

TRINOVANTES

DOBUNNI   CATUVELLAUNI

DEMETAE

SILURES

ATREBATES   CANTIACI

DUROTRIGES

DUMNONII

Grassy ramparts and ditches of the Iron Age hillfort Maiden Castle, Dorset. At its apogee, around 450 BC, Maiden Castle was the largest of its kind, its sevenfold rampart enclosing an area the size of 19 hectares (47 acres) – the equivalent of 19 rugby pitches – and home to several hundred people. Though it was still being utilized at the time of the Claudian invasion, around 100 BC the habitation had gone into decline, with the western half of the hillfort being abandoned. Today, the ramparts look smooth and sinuous, but the original fortification would have been built up with massive, box-like timber revetments, stockades, walls and all manner of obstacles. The intention was to impress as much as secure. (ian freeman/Wikimedia Commons/ CC-BY-SA-3.0)

II Augusta departed Alchester around AD 60. If the average age of legionary recruits ranged between 17 and 25 years of age, and the standard length of service for a legionary was 25 years, then Lucius Valerius signed up during the middle years of Tiberius' reign (AD 14–37). The base of Legio II Augusta at that time was Argentoratum–Strasbourg, from which he may have taken part in the Germanic follies of Caius Caligula across the Rhenus. Three years later, Lucius Valerius was fighting in Britannia under Vespasianus.

The legionary fortress at Alchester must have been constructed earlier, and probably in the year of invasion, which would make it the earliest of its kind in Roman Britain and the headquarters of its current *legatus legionis*, Vespasianus, during the legion's campaign in the south-west.

The Maiden Castle myth

The belief that Legio II Augusta brought about the devastating demise of Maiden Castle with the use of iron-shod *ballistae* bolts is a myth, which is sad to say because it is a potent (almost iconic) story that still captures the imagination of academics and the public alike. Simply put, the Maiden Castle myth all dates back to Mortimer Wheeler (1890–1976), who, during his fieldwork of 1936–37, interpreted a series of burials found in the east gate of the hillfort as a 'war cemetery'.

A firm adherent of what today is termed historical archaeology, Wheeler saw this Iron Age cemetery as evidence of the furious but futile resistance, in the face of Roman aggression, by the local Durotriges tribe. The most famous of the 52 or so skeletons recovered was the adult male (Skeleton PA7) with an iron projectile lodged in his spine (Wheeler 1943, pp. 62–63, 352–53). The leaf-shaped blade is in fact a spearhead or javelin point rather than the more frequently stated *ballista* bolt, which usually had a pyramidal bodkin head, and is possibly even of indigenous fabrication (Russell 2019, p. 329). Amidst all this, the hillfort had, it would appear, been largely abandoned by the early 1st century AD, which might indicate why it was not reused by Legio II Augusta in the immediate aftermath of the campaign, as was the case with Hod Hill (Stewart and Russell 2017, pp. 158–62).

AFTERMATH

As noted, 11 tribal leaders are said to have made capitulation to Claudius at Camulodunum–Colchester, but the only tribe whose submission is recorded is that mentioned in passing by Cassius Dio when he says Aulus Plautius had 'won over a section of the Bodounni [viz. Dobunni], who were subject to the Catuvellauni' (60.20.2). These Britons were likely members of the northern Dobunni, and may have been a tribal contingent serving under Togodumnus and Caratacus. Cassius Dio also tells us that Claudius 'deprived those who submitted of their arms' and handed them over to Aulus Plautius, ordering 'him to subdue the remaining areas' (60.21.5). In all probability, the 11 tribes belonged to the area of Britannia under current occupation, and they were certainly unlikely at this stage of the game to include any beyond the frontier zone.

Presumably, Aulus Plautius understood what the emperor meant by his instructions to him, but they are opaque to us. Did 'the remaining areas' mean the rest of Britannia, or only what had been previously determined? Later events suggest that while the long-term aim was total conquest, the

Colchester Castle, Colchester, Essex. Established a year or so after the Roman occupation, Camulodunum–Colchester became the main centre of the new regime with Legio XX in residence. The castle itself stands foursquare upon the remains of the lofty podium of a massive temple 'erected to the divine Claudius' (Tac. *Ann.* 14.31.3). Completed by around 1100, the Norman builders also took tiles and stone from this and the ruins of other Roman buildings in the vicinity. (M. Baker/Wikimedia Commons/ Public Domain)

Camulodunum–Colchester before and after AD 43

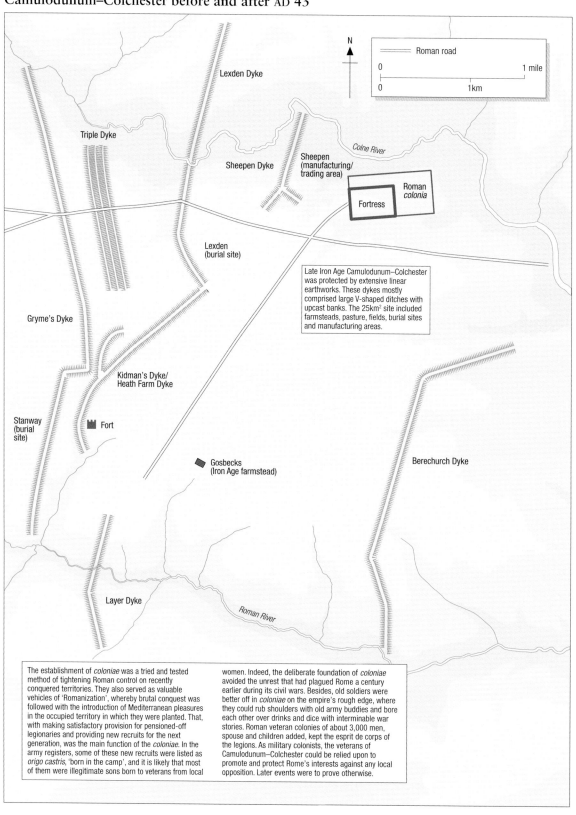

N

Roman road

0   1 mile

0   1km

Lexden Dyke

Triple Dyke

Colne River

Sheepen Dyke

Sheepen
(manufacturing/
trading area)

Roman
colonia

Fortress

Lexden
(burial site)

Late Iron Age Camulodunum–Colchester
was protected by extensive linear
earthworks. These dykes mostly
comprised large V-shaped ditches with
upcast banks. The 25km² site included
farmsteads, pasture, fields, burial sites
and manufacturing areas.

Gryme's Dyke

Kidman's Dyke/
Heath Farm Dyke

Stanway
(burial
site)

Fort

Gosbecks
(Iron Age farmstead)

Berechurch Dyke

Layer Dyke

Roman River

The establishment of *coloniae* was a tried and tested
method of tightening Roman control on recently
conquered territories. They also served as valuable
vehicles of 'Romanization', whereby brutal conquest was
followed with the introduction of Mediterranean pleasures
in the occupied territory in which they were planted. That,
with making satisfactory provision for pensioned-off
legionaries and providing new recruits for the next
generation, was the main function of the *coloniae*. In the
army registers, some of these new recruits were listed as
origo castris, 'born in the camp', and it is likely that most
of them were illegitimate sons born to veterans from local
women. Indeed, the deliberate foundation of *coloniae*
avoided the unrest that had plagued Rome a century
earlier during its civil wars. Besides, old soldiers were
better off in *coloniae* on the empire's rough edge, where
they could rub shoulders with old army buddies and bore
each other over drinks and dice with interminable war
stories. Roman veteran colonies of about 3,000 men,
spouse and children added, kept the esprit de corps of
the legions. As military colonists, the veterans of
Camulodunum–Colchester could be relied upon to
promote and protect Rome's interests against any local
opposition. Later events were to prove otherwise.

first stage was the subjugation of the tribes of south-east Britannia and their incorporation into a province. It is from Tacitus we learn that under the first two governors, Aulus Plautius (AD 43–47) and Publius Ostorius Scapula (AD 47–51), 'both distinguished soldiers':

> The nearest portion of Britannia [*proxima pars Britanniae*] was reduced little by little to the condition of a province [*in formam provinciae*]; a colony of veterans was also planted. (Tac. *Agr.* 14.1)

That veteran colony was the ill-fated Camulodunum–Colchester. In another place, Tacitus (*Ann.* 12.32) indicates that when Colonia Camulodunum was founded in AD 50, it was to take over from Legio II Augusta the function of surveillance (*subsidium adversus rebellis*) of the subjugated tribes and act as a means of familiarizing them with law-abiding government (*ad officia legum*).

Actually, the brutality of the Romans was as solid as their imperial infrastructure, and a decade later the symbol of Roman occupation that the veteran colony came to represent was to be a prime cause of the Boudican rebellion, which all but swept the Romans from Britannia. As Tacitus lets on, if it had not been for the rapid response of the then serving governor, Suetonius Paulinus, *amissa Britannia foret*, 'Britannia would have been lost' (*Agr.* 16.2).

CONQUERED FOR VANITY

But was the agony of conquest, occupation and consolidation really worth it? After all, the Roman modus operandi was primarily to exploit the wealth of a province. The Greek-speaking Strabo wrote the finest work we possess on the political geography of the Roman Empire in his day. In a passage (4.5.3) concerning distant Britannia, as that land of mystery was known to the Mediterranean world, but called Albion by its inhabitants, he explains why it was useless to conquer lands with poor resources; that is to say, keeping them would soon outstrip any

The Roman Empire at the death of Claudius

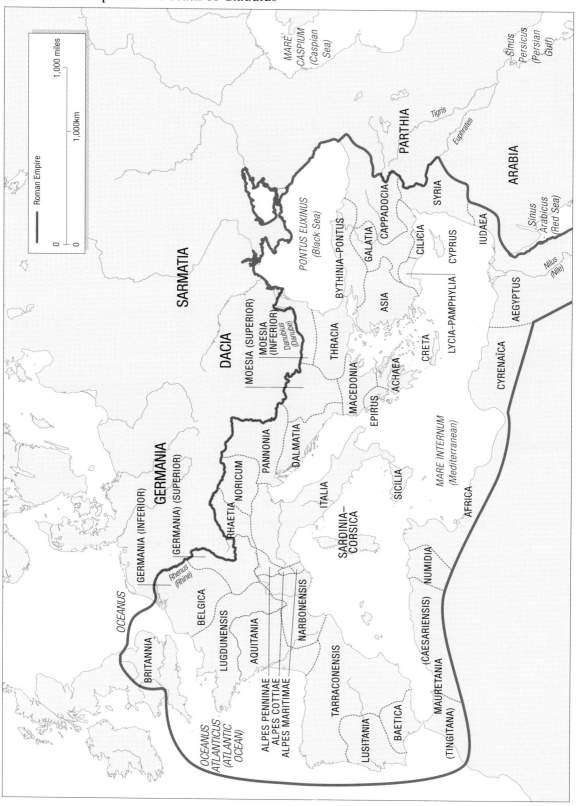

1,000 miles

1,000km

Roman Empire

MARE CASPIUM (Caspian Sea)

Sinus Persicus (Persian Gulf)

PARTHIA

Tigris

Euphrates

ARABIA

SARMATIA

CAPPADOCIA

SYRIA

PONTUS EUXINUS (Black Sea)

BYTHINIA–PONTUS

GALATIA

CILICIA

CYPRUS

IUDAEA

Sinus Arabicus (Red Sea)

Nilus (Nile)

ASIA

LYCIA-PAMPHYLIA

AEGYPTUS

THRACIA

CRETA

DACIA

MOESIA (SUPERIOR)

MOESIA (INFERIOR)

Danubius (Danube)

MACEDONIA

ACHAEA

CYRENAÏCA

MOESIA (SUPERIOR)

EPIRUS

MARE INTERNUM (Mediterranean)

PANNONIA

DALMATIA

NORICUM

RHAETIA

ITALIA

SICILIA

AFRICA

GERMANIA

GERMANIA (INFERIOR)

(GERMANIA) (SUPERIOR)

SARDINIA– CORSICA

NUMIDIA

OCEANUS

Rhenus (Rhine)

BELGICA

LUGDUNENSIS

AQUITANIA

NARBONENSIS

ALPES PENNINAE
ALPES COTTIAE
ALPES MARITIMAE

(CAESARIENSIS)

BRITANNIA

TARRACONENSIS

MAURETANIA

OCEANUS ATLANTICUS (ATLANTIC OCEAN)

LUSITANIA

BAETICA

(TINGITANA)

economic benefits. Britannia certainly did not (and still does not) enjoy an exceedingly mild climate that allows the vine, the olive, the laurel, the pomegranate and all the other fruits a Mediterranean sky allows to come to perfection. Strabo was writing in the age of Augustus, and of course we are faced with the ironic fact that the Claudian adventure of AD 43, and the expansionist campaigns that followed in Britannia, meant the Romans nevertheless were to occupy a large chunk of the mainland island, and thus added a province beyond what was considered the natural bounds of the empire.

At no time, of course, during the Roman occupation of Britannia did the military extend control over the whole of the mainland island. The northern part proved more difficult to dominate. The terrain was harder, the winters were harsher and the logistics an out-and-out headache. This was in a very real sense a case of a province too far. This was a truism that Augustus himself had fully recognized, and, despite being Caesar's heir, he had rejected the option of invasion. Besides, during his principate, Britannic kings were already paying honours to Augustus and making offerings on the Capitol (Strab. 2.5.8, 4.5.3). And let us not forget the attitude to Britannia of Nero, who surely has gone down in history as one of the worst emperors:

> He was never at any time moved by any desire or hope of expanding the empire. He even considered withdrawing the army from Britannia, and only desisted from his purpose because he did not wish to appear to belittle the glory of his (adoptive) father [Claudius, now deified]. (Suet. *Ner.* 18)

This was a negative sentiment that probably suggested itself to the emperor during the Boudican rebellion, or in the uncertain climate of its aftermath. Whenever it was, this outlook conveyed the view that the then world superpower was ready to cut and run.

The occupation of Britannia in AD 43 was a distraction from the political discomfiture of Claudius' accession and uncertainties of his first two years as emperor. It is not that wiser heads in Rome had revised their view of the value of the country, and the conviction that Britannia was not worth its salt lingered on. Appian of Alexandria, who, as a former financial secretary to Antoninus Pius (r. AD 138–61) – the emperor who ordered the building of the turf wall that bears his name – had sound knowledge of the cost of empire building, would later summarize in a few words what must by now have become apparent, that the 'Romans already have the best part of Britannia and do not need the rest, for even the part they have profits them nothing' (*Romaïká praefatio* 5). Just as Cassius Dio, with Greek tongue-in-cheek, remarks about an officer who had been unsparingly reprimanded, 'Lucius Verus did not put him to death, but merely sent him to Britannia' (72.14). It almost seems as if Britannia was barren, outlaw and Rome's symbolic 'other'. The Claudian invasion of Britannia was a happenstance of hope, its aims absurd, no more than a quest for glory. It was a misguided enterprise, and the province itself was to prove a rather expensive mistake. But like most expensive mistakes made in the name of so-called good governance, when it came to admitting to the truth of the matter, the theory of inverse validity took centre stage.

AN AFTERTHOUGHT

For all its majesty and authority, the universal peace imposed by Rome, what we call Pax Romana, would not outlive the 2nd century AD. We see it, from the advantage of hindsight, as an extended respite from the gruesome norms of human conduct. On the whole, the Roman provinces had enjoyed stable and orderly government, and the frontiers of the empire were made comparatively safe. However, even if two predominately peaceful and prosperous centuries were a formidable achievement, the effect would be to pond up external pressures that one day would overflow. In the meantime, Rome's enemies were getting stronger. Iron Age man had little taste for order, let alone domination by another, and did not like being reminded how much power another had over him. This was not the natural order.

> I had men and horses, arms and wealth. What wonder if I parted with them reluctantly? If you Romans choose to lord it over the world, does it follow that the world is to accept slavery? (Caratacus, in Tac. *Ann*. 12.36)

Seized and sent to Rome in chains, where he was to be pardoned by Claudius, Caratacus asked a question of imperialism famous for its irony: 'You have so much; why do you covet our poor huts?' (Dio 61.33.3). It was inevitable that 'barbarians' should stress Roman greed. *Raptores orbis*, 'globe grabbers' (Tac. *Agr*. 30.4), bellows a Caledonii war leader. He continues:

> Plunder, murder and rapine, these things they misname empire: they create desolation and call it peace. (Calgacus, in Tac. *Agr*. 30.5)

Tacitus, despite being an arch imperialist, was also one of the most powerful critics of the imperial project. Thus, it is highly doubtful whether either Caratacus or Calgacus really said these things, but the sentiment is highly plausible nevertheless.

Roman imperialism was concerned not with poor huts, but rich fields. The pre-battle harangue of Boudica offers as much when she says of the legions facing her rebel army: 'They cannot do without bread, wine and oil; and if just one of these should fail, so will they' (Dio 62.5.5). Predictably, in the eyes of our valiant warrior queen, those same legions personify nothing more than oriental servitude and Roman decadence:

> I am queen not of toiling Egyptians as was Nitocris or money-grovelling Assyrians as was Semiramis ... I beseech the Gods for victory against these insolent and insatiable men – if those who take warm baths, eat sweetmeats, drink wine un-watered, smear themselves with scent and lie with boys on soft couches deserve the name of men! They who are lackeys to a lyre player [viz. Nero] – and a bloody awful one at that! (Boudica, in Dio 62.6.2, 4)

The Roman occupation of Britannia was just that – an occupation. It was a temporary presence, albeit an influential one.

GLOSSARY AND ABBREVIATIONS

Adiutrix pia fidelis — 'Supportive'

ala (pl. *alae*) — 'wing' – *auxilia* (q.v.) cavalry unit

Alaudae — 'Larks' – levied in Gallia Cisalpina

aquila — 'eagle' – eagle-standard of *legio* (q.v.), its most precious possession

aquilifer (pl. *aquiliferi*) — 'eagle-bearer' – senior standard-bearer who carried *aquila* (q.v.)

armilla (pl. *armillae*) — 'armband' – military decorations

as (pl. *asses*) — Roman copper coin, originally worth one-tenth of *denarius* (q.v.), but revaluated 16 to the *denarius* at the time of the Gracchi

Augusta — 'Augustan' – reconstituted by Augustus

aureus (pl. *aurei*) — Roman gold coin valued at 25 silver *denarii* (q.v.)

auxilia — 'supports' – auxiliary units made up of *peregrini* (q.v.)

caliga (pl. *caligae*) — hobnailed footwear of Roman soldiers of the rank of *centurio* (q.v.) down

centuria (pl. *centuriae*) — basic sub-unit of *cohors* (q.v.)

centurio (pl. *centuriones*) — 'leader of one hundred' – officer in command of *centuria* (q.v.)

cingulum (pl. *cinguli*) — military belt

clipeus (pl. *clipi*) — shield used by *auxilia* (q.v.)

cohors (pl. *cohortes*) — 1. basic operational unit of *legio* (q.v.) 2. independent unit of *auxilia* (q.v.)

cohors equitata — part-mounted unit of *auxilia* (q.v.) unit

commentarius (pl. *commentarii*) — note to assist memory, memorandum

contubernium — 'tentful' – mess-unit of eight infantry, ten per *centuria* (q.v.)

corona — 'crown' – military decoration

cornicen (pl. *cornicines*) — musician who blew *cornu*, a horn associated with standards

cos. — consul

decurio (pl. *decuriones*) — officer in command of *turma* (q.v.)

denarius (pl. *denarii*) — 'ten as piece' – Roman silver coin 4g in weight and valued at 16 *asses*/four *sesterces* (q.v.)

duplicarius — second-in-command of *turma* (q.v.)

Equestris — 'Mounted'

Fulminata — 'equipped with the thunderbolt'

gladius (pl. *gladii*) — cut-and-thrust sword carried by Roman soldiers

Gemina — 'Twin' – one legion made out of two

Gk. — Greek

Hispana — 'Iberian' – served in Iberia

imperium — power to command

La Tène — 'the shallows' – Iron Age culture named after site at La Tène, Lac de Neuchâtel in Switzerland

Lat. — Latin

legatus (pl. *legati*) — 'deputy' – man to whom the emperor delegated responsibility

legatus legionis — senatorial commander in command of *legio* (q.v.)

legio (pl. *legiones*) — principal operational unit of Roman army

lorica (pl. *loricae*) — body armour

Martia — 'sacred to Mars'

mercatores — traders

miles (pl. *militis*) — soldier

OE — Old English

oppidum (pl. *oppida*) — 'town' – large, town-like settlements of Iron Age date in Britain and on the Continent

optio (pl. *optiones*) — 'chosen' – second-in-command of *centuria* (q.v.)

ornamenta triumphalia — insignia awarded by emperor to victorious commanders

patera (pl. *paterae*) — bronze mess tin used by Roman soldiers

peregrinus (pl. *peregrini*) — non-Roman citizen

phalera (pl. *phalerae*) — 'disc' – military decoration worn on chest

pia fidelis — 'loyal and true'

pilum (pl. *pila*) — principal throwing weapon of legionaries

pl. — plural

praefectus — commander of auxiliary *cohors* (q.v.)

praefectus castrorum — third-in-command of *legio* (q.v.)

pro-consul — consul whose command was prolonged

pugio (pl. *pugiones*) — short dagger, cut down version of *gladius* (q.v.), carried by Roman soldiers

q.v. — *quod vide*, see

Rapax — 'Greedy'

rex — ruler, king

Sabina — 'Sabine' – levied in Sabine territory

scutum (pl. *scuta*) — oval body shield carried by legionaries

signifer (pl. *signiferi*) — standard-bearer

suff. cos. — *consul suffectus* – consul appointed to complete the year of a consul who resigned, died or was incapacitated.

topos — theme, topic

torque (pl. *torques*) — 'neckband' – 1. Celtic status symbol ornament 2. Roman military decoration

tribunus (pl. *tribuni*) — senior officers serving under *legatus legionis* (q.v.)

turma (pl. *turmae*) — basic sub-unit of *ala* (q.v.)

umbo (pl. *umbones*) — boss of shield, usually metallic

Valeria — 'Powerful'

vexillatio (pl. *vexillationes*) — detachment from one or more legions

Victrix — 'Victorious'

vitis — twisted vine-stick carried by *centurio* (q.v.)

BIBLIOGRAPHY

Barrett, A.A., Caligula: *The Corruption of Power*, London: Guild Publishing, 1989

——, 'Chronological Errors in Dio's Account of the Claudian Invasion', *Britannia*, 11, 1990, pp. 31–33

——, 'Claudius' British Victory Arch in Rome', *Britannia*, 22, 1991, pp. 1–21

——, 'The Date of Claudius' British Campaign', *Classical Quarterly*, 48/2, 1998, pp. 574–77

Bédoyère, G. de la, *Eagles Over Britannia: The Roman Army in Britain*, Stroud: Tempus Publishing, 2001

——, *Defying Rome: The Rebels of Roman Britain*, Stroud: Tempus, 2003

Belloc, H., *The Old Road*, London: Constable & Co., 1911 [1904]

Bird, D.G., 'The Claudian Invasion Campaign Reconsidered', *Oxford Journal of Archaeology*, 19/1, 2000, pp. 91–104

Birley, A.R., *The Roman Government of Britain*, Oxford: Oxford University Press, 2005

Black, E.W., 'How Many Rivers to Cross', *Britannia*, 29, 1998, pp. 306–07

Bradley, C.M., *The Ancient Britons and the Roman Invasions 55 BC–AD 60: An Analysis of Tribal Resistance and Response*, PhD thesis, Massey University, 2003

——, 'The British War Chariot: A Case for Indirect Warfare', *Journal of Military History*, 73.4, 2009, pp. 1073–89

Brewster, T.C.M., 'The Garton Slack Chariot Burial, East Yorkshire', *Antiquity*, 45, 1971, pp. 289–92

Bright, D., 'The Pilgrims' Way Revisited: The Use of the North Downs Main Trackway and the Medway Crossing by Medieval Travellers', Maidstone: Kent Archaeological Society eArticle (www.kentarchaeological.ac/authors/DerekBright01.pdf), 2010

Burn, A.R., 'The Battle of the Medway, AD 43', *History*, 38/133, 1953, pp. 105–15

Caplan, J. (ed.), *Written on the Body: The Tattoo in European and American History*, London: Reaktion Books, 2000

Campbell, J.B., *The Roman Army, 31 BC–AD 337: A Sourcebook*, London: Routledge, 1994

——, *The Emperor and the Roman Army 31 BC–AD 235*, Oxford: Clarendon Press, 1996 [1984]

Carr, G., 'Woad, Tattooing and Identity in Later Iron Age and Early Roman Britain', *Oxford Journal of Archaeology*, 24/3, 2005, pp. 273–92

Carson, R.A.G., 'The Bredgar Treasure of Roman Coins', *The Numismatic Chronicle and Journal of the Royal Numismatic Society*, 19, 1959, pp. 17–22

Creighton, J., *Britannia: The Creation of a Roman Province*, London: Routledge, 2006

Crummy, P., 'Colchester, Fortress and Colonia', *Britannia*, 8, 1977, pp. 65–106

——, *City of Victory: The Story of Colchester: Britain's First Roman Town*, Colchester: Colchester Archaeological Trust, 1997

Cunliffe, B.W., *Iron Age Communities in Britain*, 3rd edn., London: Routledge, 1991

——, *The Ancient Celts*, Oxford: Oxford University Press, 1997

——, *Fishbourne Roman Palace*, Stroud: Tempus, 1998

——, *Facing the Ocean: The Atlantic and its Peoples*, Oxford: Oxford University Press, 2001

——, *The Celts: A Very Short Introduction*, Oxford: Oxford University Press, 2003

—— and Miles, D. (eds.), *Aspects of the Iron Age in Central Southern Britain*, Oxford: Oxford University Press, 1984

Diack, F.C., Alexander, W.M. and MacDonald, J., *The Inscriptions of Pictland: An Essay on the Sculptured and Inscribed Stones of the North East and North of Scotland, with Other Writings and Collections*, Aberdeen: Third Spalding Club, 1944

Fields, N., *Roman Auxiliary Cavalryman, AD 14–193*, Oxford: Osprey Publishing, 2006 (Warrior 101)

——, *Rome's Saxon Shore: Coastal Defences of Roman Britain AD 250–500*, Oxford: Osprey Publishing, 2006 (Fortress 56)

——, *The Roman Army of the Principate 27 BC–AD 117*, Oxford: Osprey Publishing, 2009 (Battle Orders 37)

——, *Boudica's Rebellion AD 60–61: The Britons Rise Up Against Rome*, Oxford: Osprey Publishing, 2011 (Campaign 233)

Fink, R.O., *Roman Military Records on Papyrus*, New Haven: Case Western Reserve University Press, 1971

Fitzpatrick, A.P., 'Ebbsfleet, 54 BC', *Current Archaeology*, 337, 2018, pp. 26–32

——, 'Caesar's landing sites in Britain and Gaul in 55 and 54 BC: Critical Places, Natural Places', in Fitzpatrick, A.P. and Haselgrove, C. (eds.), *Julius Caesar's Battle for Gaul: New*

Archaeological Perspectives, Oxford: Oxbow Books, 2019, pp. 135–58

Frere, S.S., and Fulford, M.G., 'The Roman invasion of Britain of AD 43', *Britannia*, 32, 2001, pp. 45–56

Goldsworthy, A.K., *The Roman Army at War: 100 BC–AD 200*, Oxford: Clarendon Press, 1998

Grainge, G., *The Roman Channel Crossing of AD 43*, Oxford: Tempus Reparatum, 2002

——, *The Roman Invasions of Britain*, Stroud: Tempus, 2005

Hassall, M.W.C., 'Batavians and the Roman conquest of Britain', *Britannia*, 1, 1970, pp. 131–36

Hill, J.D., 'Wetwang Chariot Burial', *Current Archaeology*, 178, 2002, pp. 410–12

Hind, J.G F., 'The Invasion of Britain in AD 43 – an Alternative Strategy for Aulus Plautius', *Britannia*, 20, 1989, pp. 1–21

——, 'A. Plautius' Campaign in Britain: an Alternative Reading of the Narrative in Cassius Dio (60.19.5–21.2)', *Britannia*, 38, 2007, pp. 93–107

Hoffman, B., *The Roman Invasion of Britain: Archaeology versus History*, Barnsley: Pen & Sword Archaeology, 2013

James, S., *Exploring the World of the Celts*, London: Thames & Hudson, 1998 [1993]

——, *The Atlantic Celts: Ancient People or Modern Invention?*, London: British Museum Press, 1999

—— and Rigby, V., *Britain and the Celtic Iron Age*, London: British Museum Press, 1997

Jones, B., and Mattingly, D., *An Atlas of Roman Britain*, Oxford: Oxbow Books, 2002 [1990]

Jones, C.P., 'Stigma, Tattooing and Branding in Graeco-Roman Antiquity', *Journal of Roman Studies*, 87, 1987, pp. 139–55

Kaye, S.J., 'The Roman Invasion of Britain, 43 AD: Riverine, Wading and Tidal Studies Place Limits on the Possible Locations of the Two-Day River Battle and Beachhead', *Archaeologia Cantiana*, 136, 2015, pp. 227–40

Keppie, L.J.F., 'Legio VIII Augusta and the Claudian invasion', *Britannia*, 2, 1971, pp. 149–55

Le Bohec, Y, *L'armée Romaine, sous le Haut-Empire*, Paris: Les Éditions Picard, 1989

Levick, B., *Claudius*, London: Batsford, 1990

Loades, M., 'Building an Iron Age British Chariot' (www.mikeloades.com), 2002

——, 'Wetwang: A Chariot Fit for a Queen?' (www.bbc.co.uk/history/trail/archaeology/wetwang/wetwang_chariot_queen_01.shtml), 2005

MacQuarrie, C., 'Insular Celts Tattooing: History, Myth and Metaphor', *Études Celtique*, 23, 1999, pp. 159–89

Manley, J., *AD 43: The Roman Invasion of Britain, a Reassessment*, Stroud: Tempus, 2002

Peddie, J., *Invasion: The Roman Conquest of Britain*, New York: St. Martin's Press, 1987

Phillips, E.J., 'The Emperor Gaius' Abortive Invasion of Britain', *Historia: Zeitschrift für Alte Geschichte*, 19/3, 1970, pp. 369–74

Pleiner, R., *The Celtic Sword*, Oxford: Oxford University Press, 1993

Powell, T.G.E., *The Celts*, London: Thames & Hudson, 1983

Pryor, F., *Britain BC: Life in Britain and Ireland Before the Romans*, London: HarperCollins Publishers, 2003

Rankin, H.D., *Celts and the Classical World*, London: Croom Helm, 1987

Rankov, N.B., 'Fleets of the Early Roman Empire, 31 BC–AD 324', in Morrison, J.S., and Gardiner, R. (eds.), *The Age of the Galley: Mediterranean Oared Vessels since Pre-Classical Times*, London: Conway Maritime Press, 2000 [1995], pp. 78–85

Rawlings, L., 'Celts, Spaniards, and Samnites: Warriors in a Soldier's War', in Cornell, T.J., Rankov, N.B., and Sabin, P. (eds.), *The Second Punic War: A Reappraisal*, London: University of London Press, 1996

Redfern, R.C., 'A Re-appraisal of the Evidence for Violence in the Late Iron Age Human Remains from Maiden Castle Hillfort, Dorset, England', *Proceedings of the Prehistoric Society*, 77, 2011, pp. 111–38

Ritchie, W.F., and Ritchie, J.N.G., *Celtic Warriors*, Princes Risborough: Shire, 1985 (Shire Archaeology 41)

Roymans, N., *Ethnic Identity and Imperial Power: The Batavians in the Early Roman Empire*, Amsterdam: Amsterdam University Press, 2004 (Amsterdam Archaeological Studies 10)

Russell, M., 'Mythmakers of Maiden Castle: Breaking the Siege Mentality of an Iron Age Hillfort', *Oxford Journal of Archaeology*, 38/3, 2019, pp. 325–42

Salway, P., *Roman Britain*, Oxford: Clarendon Press, 1988 [1981]

——, *Roman Britain: A Very Short Introduction*, Oxford: Oxford University Press, 2000

Sauer, E.W., 'Alchester Roman Fortress', *Current Archaeology*, 173, 2001, pp. 189–91

——, 'The Roman Invasion of Britain (AD 43) in Imperial Perspective: A Response to Frere and Fulford', *Oxford Journal of Archaeology*, 21/4, 2002, pp. 333–63

——, 'Alchester: In Search of Vespasian', *Current Archaeology*, 196, 2005, pp. 168–76

Starr, C.G., Jr., *The Roman Imperial Navy, 31 BC–AD 324*, Westport, CN: Greenwood Press, 1975 [1941]

Stewart, D., and Russell, M., *Hillforts and the Durotriges: A Geophysical Survey of Iron Age Dorset*, Oxford: Archaeopress, 2017

Thornhill, P., 'The Medway Crossing of the Pilgrims' Way', *Archaeologia Cantiana*, 89, 1974, pp. 91–100

——, 'A Lower Thames Ford and the Campaigns of 54 BC and AD 43', *Archaeologia Cantiana*, 92, 1976, pp. 119–28

Webster, G., *The Roman Imperial Army of the First and Second Centuries AD*, 2nd edn., London: A & C Black, 1979

——, *The Roman Invasion of Britain*, London: Book Club Associates, 1981 [1980]

——, *Rome against Caratacus: The Roman Campaigns in Britain AD 48–58*, London: B.T. Batsford, 1993 (revised edition)

——, *Boudica: The British Revolt against Rome AD 60*, London: Routledge, 1999

Wheeler, M., *Maiden Castle, Dorset*, London: Society of Antiquaries, 1943 (Society of Antiquaries Report 12)

Williams, D., *Romans and Barbarians: Four Views from the Empire's Edge 1st Century AD*, New York: St. Martin's Press, 1999 [1998]

Abbreviations of cited authors and works

AE	*L'Année épigraphique*, Paris: Presses Universitaires de France, 1888–
Amm. Marc.	Ammianus Marcellinus
Arr.	Flavius Arrianus
Takt.	*Téchne Taktiké*
Caes.	Caesar
B civ.	*Bellum civile*
B Gall.	*Bellum Gallicum*
[Caes.]	Pseudo-Caesar
B Alex.	*Bellum Alexandrinum*
Cic.	Cicero
Att.	*Epistulae ad Atticum*
QFr.	*Epistulae ad Quintum Fratrem*
CIL	Mommsen, T., Hirschfeld, O. and Dessau, H., *Corpus Inscriptionum Latinarum*, Berlin, 1862–
Digest	Digest of Justinian
Dio	Cassius Dio
Diod. Sic.	Diodorus Siculus
Eutrp.	Flavius Eutropius
Hor.	Horace
Epod.	*Epodi*
Sat.	*Satirae*
Hyginus	Caius Julius Hyginus
ILS	Dessau, H., *Inscriptiones Latinae Selectae*, 3 vols, Berlin, 1892–1916
Isid.	Isidorus Hispalensis
Etym.	*Etymologiae*
Jor.	Jordanes
Get.	*Getica*
Joseph.	Flavius Josephus
Ant. Iud.	*Antiquitates Iudaicae*
B Iud.	*Bellum Iudaicum*
Juv.	Juvenal
Sat.	*Satirae*
Mar.	Martial
Epigr.	*Epigrammata*
Oros.	Orosius
Ov.	Ovid
Am.	*Amores*
Pan. Lat.	*XII Panegyrici Latini*
Philo	Philo Iudaeos
Leg.	*Legatio ad Caium*
Pl.	Plato
Phd.	*Phaedo*
Plin.	Pliny (the elder)
HN	*Naturalis Historia*

Polyb.	Polybios
RIB	Tomlin, R.S.O., *Roman Inscriptions of Britain*, Stroud: Alan Sutton, 1995
RIC I	Sutherland, C.H.V., *Roman Imperial Coins*, Vol. 1, London, 1984
RPC I	Burnett, A., Amandry, M., and Rippolès, P.P., *Roman Provincial Coinage*, Vol. 1, London/Paris, 2006 [1992]
Sil.	Silius Italicus
Pun.	*Punica*
Strab.	Strabo
Suet.	Suetonius
Aug.	*Divus Augustus*
Calig.	*Caius Caligula*
Claud.	*Divus Claudius*
Galb.	*Galba*
Ner.	*Nero*
Vesp.	*Divus Vespasianus*
Tac.	Tacitus
Ann.	*Annales*
Agr.	*Agricola*
Ger.	*Germania*
Hist.	*Historiae*
Veg.	Vegetius
Mil.	*De re militari*
Virg.	Virgil
Ecl.	*Eclogues*

INDEX

Figures in **bold** refer to illustrations.